The 1600 cc Abarth Carrera, one of the most sought-after and
coveted Porsches. *Greg Brown/Argus*

Motorbooks International Illustrated Buyer's Guide Series

Illustrated

PORSCHE
BUYER'S ★ GUIDE™

Dean Batchelor

Motorbooks International
Publishers & Wholesalers ®

This third edition published in 1990 by
Motorbooks International Publishers &
Wholesalers, P O Box 2, 729 Prospect Avenue,
Osceola, WI 54020 USA

Motorbooks International is a certified
trademark, registered with the United States
Patent Office

The information in this book is true and
complete to the best of our knowledge. All
recommendations are made without any
guarantee on the part of the author or
publisher, who also disclaim any liability
incurred in connection with the use of this data
or specific details

We recognize that some words, model names
and designations, for example, mentioned
herein are the property of the trademark
holder. We use them for identification purposes
only. This is not an official publication

Motorbooks International books are also
available at discounts in bulk quantity for
industrial or sales-promotional use. For details
write to Special Sales Manager at the
Publisher's address

Library of Congress Cataloging-in-Publication Data
Batchelor, Dean.
    Illustrated Porsche buyer's guide / Dean Batchelor.
        p. cm.
    ISBN 0-87938-435-2
    1. Porsche automobile—Purchasing.
    I. Title. II. Series
TL215.P75B37 1990   89-28174
629.222'2—dc20   CIP

On the front cover: The 1978 911SC Porsche
painted in Petrol Blue and owned by Bill
Caldwell of White Bear Lake, Minnesota. *Gordon
Maltby*

On the back cover: The 1990 Porsche 944 S2
Cabriolet. *Porsche*

Printed and bound in the United States of
America

Contents

Credits and Acknowledgments

I want to express my sincere and grateful thanks to those who gave time, information, technical assistance, or furnished photos, to aid in the creation of this book: Argus Publishers Corporation; Frank Barrett; Tom Birch; Greg Brown, *VW & Porsche;* Larry Brown, Porsche+Audi; Gary Emory, Porsche Parts Obsolete; Brett Johnson, PB Tweeks; Bill Jones, Jones' Autowerkes; Fred Heyler, Porsche+Audi; Martha McKinley, PCNA; Don Orosco; Jim Perrin; Rudi Spielberger, Porsche+Audi; Chuck Stoddard, Stoddard Imported Cars, Inc.; Vic Skirmants; Betty Jo Turner, *Porsche Panorama;* Dr. Leonard Turner; Robert Wood, Robert W. Wood, Inc.; *Road & Track* library.

And to those who allowed me to photograph their cars: Gene Gilpin, Harrah's Automobile Collection, Brian Kleeman, Bill Motta, Bob Raucher, Carter Robinson, Steve Sailors, Dean Watts.

Dean Batchelor

Introduction

Porsche fever has got you, right? You see the beautiful people zipping around in those squat, racy-looking coupes with five-thousand-dollar paint jobs and raucous exhausts that make them sound like they've just finished twenty-four hours at Le Mans. Maybe you've been passed on a winding road by a road-hugging coupe that has wheels and tires that look too big for the car, and on the rear sloping deck is a strange-looking device (looks sort of like the tail of a whale) that's large enough to be a picnic table.

Or you're sitting in your car at a stop signal and a low-slung coupe pulls alongside. You can't decide which to admire first, the car or the driver. (Porsches always seem to be driven by, or have as a passenger, a beautiful woman—they go together somehow.)

Maybe you've been to Sebring, Riverside, Elkhart Lake, Road Atlanta, LeMans or the Nürburgring and seen Porsches in action—very often in the winner's circle.

Never mind what prompted you, you're finally ready to make your move, but you aren't 100 percent sure you know the best way to do it. I'm not sure there is a "best way" but I'll do what I can to help you make the right decision.

One thing to get straight right at the start is that even though you may have located a car you want—through a friend or an advertisement in a magazine or newspaper—you don't have to be in a hurry. That car you've located may not still be available next month, next week or even tomorrow, but that

doesn't mean you have to buy it today either. It *is* possible you would miss the greatest bargain of all time, but it's also possible (and may even be probable) the car is a disaster and to jump into the deal without sufficient knowledge could be the costliest automotive investment mistake you'll ever make.

The Porsche company has been building cars since 1949, and by the end of 1989 had produced about 770,000 cars. About half were sold in the European, United Kingdom and Australasian markets; about half went to the United States. Half the U.S. deliveries ended up on the West Coast, primarily in Southern California. This is advantageous to the American looking for a used Porsche because the roads and climate in California are so good that automobiles live longer and there should be a substantial number of serviceable and easily restorable Porsches available. This is important, because the earlier models have severe rust problems (more on this later).

At this point I should say that research and thorough preparation will be your biggest assets (along with money) in buying the right car. At the back of this book are lists of Porsche clubs, magazines that carry features about Porsches on a regular basis, selected books about Porsches and sources for service and hard-to-get parts.

A tremendous cottage industry has sprung up in the last few years with persons specializing in certain models; 356, 911/912, 914 or the later front-engined, water-cooled models. The specialization goes even further with those who work only on the four-cam, four-cylinder engines, or do only upholstery, or only metal work, or painting. There are stores that have bought up all the old stocks of Porsche parts they can get their hands on, and a few of them are manufacturing repro parts and accessories.

Finding a used Porsche to buy is not difficult. Finding a rare or special model probably *will* be difficult. The major newspapers in the larger U.S. cities such as New York, Los Angeles, Houston, Dallas, Atlanta, Miami, San Francisco, Boston, Chicago or Detroit should all have Porsches offered through their classified advertising section. Specialty automotive publications such as *Road & Track, AutoWeek, Hemmings Motor News* or *Old Cars Weekly,* in the U.S., or *Autocar, Autosport, Motor, Motor Sport, Motoring News, Classic and Sports Cars* or *Thoroughbred and Classic Cars,* in England, are all excellent sources. *Das Auto Motor und Sport,* in Germany, *l'Auto Journal* and *le Fanatique de l'Automobile,* in France, should also be good sources (Porsche produced cars for the British and Australasian markets, so don't fail to find out which side the steering wheel is on).

The ads placed in these publications may or may not be accurate, and you're at their mercy (caveat emptor) unless you've done your homework. Ads in Porsche club publications, and they all carry ads for cars or parts for sale, are better in many ways. The car may not be priced right, but it should be pretty much as described because the seller is reaching a knowledgeable audience (one which may know more about the car than he does), many of whom are his friends and acquaintances.

You can just about forget the "bargain" Porsche, or the one you think you can "steal" from some pigeon who doesn't know what he or she has. It still happens, but it's so rare that you can safely discount the probability of it happening to you. Apocryphal stories such as the one about the divorcee who's advertised a low-mileage 911SC in mint condition for $100 (because her ex-husband told her to sell the car and send him half the money) abound; and if you believe *that* nonsense, I have a "waterfront" lot in Florida I'd like to sell you. . . .

So, to acquire the Porsche of your dreams, you must learn as much as you can about Porsches—particularly the years and models that are close to the one you want. If your heart is set on an early 356, there's no reason to go overboard researching the 900 series cars. And if you prefer a later model then you can skip research on the earlier cars. All that can come later if you decide you want to know all there is to know about the company and its cars. Save yourself time and money by pinpointing your research toward the model you want. If you don't know yet which model you do want, then read on. The *Illustrated Porsche Buyer's Guide* can be considered a primer, as you'll get the basic information about each model built, and you can then zero in on your target car.

Even limiting the research to one model or one type can be time-consuming, and you can count on spending $300 or more on books and other literature, just on a limited area of Porsche information. But this is a drop in the bucket when compared to what you'll spend on the car, and thorough research can save you far more money than the research material cost you. If you bought every book, brochure or magazine with Porsche features you could spend in the neighborhood of $4,000.

That's the good news about Porsche books. Now for the bad news. You'll note that my recommended list of Porsche books isn't very long, considering the number of books that has been published about the marque. This is because I've found, while doing research for this book, that the vast majority of Porsche books are not accurate enough to use for research. They all contain some good information, and some good-to-excellent photos or artwork, but forget most of them for total accuracy.

I invested a great deal of money and time buying and reading some of the books left off my list when I started research for this book before I discovered them to be worthless for my purposes. If you find a book you think you want to buy but aren't sure about, ask a member of one of the Porsche clubs. Chances are he or she has at least seen them all, if not actually read them all. The avid car nut, no matter what make he likes, will often buy every book published about his favorite cars simply to have that photo or bit of information he didn't see elsewhere. He'll know the right books to buy.

Unfortunately, some of the information published by the Porsche factory or the distributor is confusing because it contradicts some other bit of information also published by the company.

Like many other car companies, Porsche may designate its components for a particular model year, but the parts may appear on an earlier or later car because they were on the shelf when a particular car went through the assembly process. This is not a prevalent situation, and the quantity of "odd" bits on a car is low, but it did happen often enough to cause argument among Porsche "experts" about a certain part being right or wrong. These odd parts don't make the particular vehicle any better or any worse, just different. And they don't make it any less desirable.

One of the major problems I've had in researching this book was to determine just when a certain mechanical change was made. Many of the sources you'll find won't tell you if they're using the calendar year or the model year.

This particular type of information is all academic to the buyer who simply wants to drive the car and enjoy it, with no intention of attempting to restore it to factory original or to show it at a Concours d'Elegance. Enthusiasts are strongly divided on this and there are good points to be made for either side.

There are enough Porsches, of all years, all models and all body styles, left in the world so that I don't see anything wrong with installing disc brakes on a non-disc-brake model, or later wheels, or even a different engine. If there were only three of a certain model left, and two were in museums and you had the third, then you would probably want to keep it original. It would be worth more, and should be preserved anyway.

Along with deciding which year, model and body style you want, and whether the car is to be for driving or for show, you will need to know who is going to work on it. Will you do it, or take it to someone else? Unless you already know quite a bit about the mechanical make-up of a Porsche, you should probably join a club. I am not a "joiner" but in this case it makes sense because if you need to find a mechanic, painter, upholsterer or simply a good place to have the car serviced, chances are pretty good the members of a Porsche club will know all the good, and bad, mechanics in the area. And if you plan to work on the car yourself, these same clubs will also have members who have done a lot of their own work and can help you.

Porsches, Ferraris, Maseratis and the like seem intimidating to the uninitiated, but if you have the right tools, a place to work on the car and have a basic understanding of an automobile's components, you can do it. I have friends who have overhauled a Porsche or Ferrari engine with excellent results, due in part to being very careful when they dismantled and then reassembled the engine. I also know some professional mechanics whom I wouldn't take a car to—any car, never mind something a bit out of the ordinary.

If you have owned Porsches, or some other sports-type car, you will probably understand the advantages and disadvantages of owning and maintaining a car that is a bit out of the norm for parts, service and driving.

Anyone who buys a Porsche should understand that it is a car that needs constant care and attention, and if properly maintained will be a joy to drive and probably as reliable as anything else on the road. Without this attention and careful maintenance, a Porsche could strand you in a terribly inconvenient spot, and then cost a bundle to fix once it's in the shop. But then, so could a lot of other cars that wouldn't be half as much fun to drive.

There's also the investment angle. Porsches are becoming more valuable and, although the early Porsches haven't caught up to early Ferraris for cost or value, they are therefore easier to buy, and still less expensive to restore than the Italian V-12.

And now a few words about a subject that is important to anyone considering the purchase of a used Porsche—rust and corrosion.

The unique design and unusual method of construction that make a Porsche a great automobile are also factors that may cause certain areas of the vehicle to be extremely susceptible to rust and deterioration. Obviously, older cars, and ones that live in areas where salt air and humidity are prevalent, are top candidates for rust. Also, those cars driven in areas where salt is used to melt ice from the roads in winter should be suspect, although most Porsche owners I know won't take their cars out in the winter in those areas.

On all 356 series cars, give the underside a very careful inspection. Start at the rear suspension torsion bar support tube that's attached to the floor or chassis pan (it's located in front and to the inside of each rear wheel). Inspect the box section where the tube is attached and move forward observing the floor from both under and inside the car. Lift up or remove the front and rear floor mats. Inspect carefully in the areas where the floor pan meets the vertical bulkheads, and also where the pan is spot-welded to the outer thresholds and the center tunnel. It is important to know:
1. Is the floor pan original, solid and intact?
2. Or has it been replaced?
3. Will it need to be replaced or repaired?

Next, look at the longitudinal panels and jacking point spurs. These are the long panels that run along the outside of the floor pan between the front and rear wheels. They house the heating tubes that conduct warm air from the engine heat exchangers to the inside of the car, and support the jack points; two on each side of the car. These panels must be in excellent condition to do their job, which provides much of the car's rigidity.

Next, open the front hood and remove the spare tire so you can inspect the front battery pan. Look at it from both inside and under the nose. Even though this area is not as critical as the floor pan, it is important that you check for the same three points listed above.

Directly behind the battery pan are the front suspension torsion bar tubes. These were jig-welded into a fabricated box section. Close inspection for rust, corrosion and previous accident damage is extremely important in this area.

Now open each door and inspect its bottom. If you don't have the car on a hoist, this will mean getting down on your knees; so, unless you're wearing your grubbies, bring along a cloth or piece of paper to kneel on. This area is important because rust repair on a 356 is very time-consuming (read expensive) if done properly. I emphasize this on the 356 because all cars of this series were virtually handmade and each hinged panel (doors, front and rear lids) was hand-fitted and leaded to fit its own opening, then serial numbered to that particular body.

In other words, interchangeability with another 356 is almost impossible (without more hand-fitting and leading) if you want to maintain correct fit—gaps and contours—between body and hinged panel. This also means that even a brand new door or hood panel, if you're fortunate enough to find one, probably won't fit properly until it has been fit to the body.

All production Porsches of the 356 series were given a factory undercoating treatment that served as a sound deadener and protective undercoat over the bare metal. Unfortunately, it did a better job of dampening sound than of protecting the metal from rust. I urge you to be very careful while inspecting any area of a 356 where undercoating has been applied, especially fresh undercoat, as it could be a coating over good solid metal or it could be covering and hiding rusty metal.

The same areas need to be inspected on 900 series Porsches as on the 356 series. It will probably be easier to spot a rusty area on a 911 than it is on a 356 series car, and repairs are easier to make because the 900 series cars have some removable and interchangeable body panels. The 900 doors are still gapped by leading, but the front and rear hoods are not, and it is possible to interchange 911 panels from one car to another of the same year and model and still achieve a good fit. This applies to the removable front fenders of all 900 series cars.

Once you've found the Porsche you think you want to buy, try to find a similar car in either original or excellent restored condition to examine so you'll have something to compare your prize to. If that can't be done, try to take a knowledgeable Porsche enthusiast with you to examine your "new" car.

Better yet, insist on taking the car to a good mechanic for a thorough checkup. If the seller is convinced you're sincere, he shouldn't object to an inspection unless he has something to hide. It's your money, and it'll be your car to live with, good or bad.

At this point I can probably alienate most avid Porsche fanatics, but at the risk of being the target of the tar-and-feather brigade I may also save you some time and money. If you're undecided about what year Porsche to buy, consider an older one for investment or for show, and a newer one for driving. When I say older, I'm talking about road cars, not race cars (those are almost always good investments). A race car will be far more costly to buy, and may be more costly to restore, but it'll also be worth more in the end.

Porsches have mystique (as do Ferraris, Bugattis, pre-World War II Alfa Romeos, pre-Rolls-Royce Bentleys, and Mercedes-Benz SS, SSK, and SSKL), but not all Porsches are great cars. All the 356 series were ill-handling beasts in my opinion (the older they are, the worse they are), and have few qualities that recommend them for everyday driving. Wider-based wheels help, as do higher tire pressures at the back than at the front. And a camber compensator at the rear is a good addition; but no matter what is done to a 356, 356A, 356B, 356C or 356 Carrera—particularly a Carrera 2—it will not give you the handling, safety or comfort of the later Porsches.

The next question from the audience is: "If the early Porsches were really that bad, how did they achieve such a great reputation?" The answer is by comparison to their contemporaries. When the first Porsches were built, the buyer of a sports car had few choices: MG TC and later the TD and TF, Singer, Triumph TR-2 and 3, Jaguar XK-120, Jowett Jupiter or . . . Porsche. A few buyers were aware of Ferraris and Aston Martins, but most had never heard of those marques, let alone seen or driven one.

When an early Porsche, as poor a handling car as it was, is compared to its contemporaries it comes off pretty well. It cost more than all but the Jaguar, Aston Martin or Ferrari, but it delivered performance that made it outstanding at the time. The speed, comfort, silence (once under way) and passenger room were unobtainable elsewhere at the price, and the Porsche was a gas miser compared to anything else—with or without the performance. But all these attributes have since been surpassed by most other cars, particularly by Porsche itself, and the early Porsche ride and handling simply are not satisfactory by today's standards.

This is not to say that an early 356 would be unbearable, but the potential buyer must understand that he or she would be getting a rather crude automobile by *today's* Porsche standards. If this is acceptable, and you can live with it, go for it. But you should drive one before you pay your money. Actually, one should drive any car before buying it.

Investment rating

★★★★★ The best. Highest prices, highest values, and best probability of further appreciation. Rarely would you find these advertised in a magazine or newspaper. Most Porsches in this group are sold or traded back and forth between knowledgeable enthusiasts. Prices will probably be in the six-figure bracket.

★★★★ Almost the best. The investment potential is good, and these should be more obtainable than the five-star cars. Like the five-star models, though, these are probably not cars you'll want to drive on the street because of their value or vulnerability. Prices will be in the high five-figure area.

★★★ Excellent value. These Porsches are highly desirable cars among Porsche enthusiasts for being driveable yet collectible. The value increase will be somewhat less than the first two groups, but because they are more affordable, there should be a reasonably good selection from which to choose.

★★ Good cars to drive and enjoy. The lower rating is mainly because of the quantity produced, making them less likely to greatly increase in value. The look, the feel, the quality is comparable to other Porsches, but they haven't made their mark on the collector as yet.

★ Well, it's a Porsche. It may have a VW engine, or a Porsche engine that's wrong for the car. Or it could be in such terrible condition that it will cost more to restore it than it will ever be worth. A one-star value Porsche could be almost any model year or body type so this is more a condition rating than a "class" or "type" rating.

Note: Add ten to twenty percent over closed-car values for open cars; Cabriolet, Speedster, Roadster in 356 series, all models, and early 911/912 "soft" back-window Targas. Also, Gmünd-built cars should be rated at five stars because of rarity and historical significance. Stuttgart-built 1950 models are three-star cars if totally original. This rating system only compares Porsches to Porsches.

Chapter 1

How it all began

The first car to bear the Porsche name, a two-passenger sports car, came about as much by chance as by some great plan.

In 1947, Porsche Konstruktionen GmbH, in Gmünd, Austria, was being run by Ferry Porsche, his sister Louise Piech, Karl Rabe and Hans Kern—the latter two, longtime associates of Ferry's father, Dr. Prof. Ferdinand Porsche. The firm's primary business was technical design and consultation.

Carlo Abarth, an Austrian former-motorcycle racer then living in Merano, Italy, began corresponding with Louise Piech (Abarth's wife had been Louise's husband Anton's secretary before World War II). Soon Ferry Porsche was drawn into the correspondence, as was another Austrian living in Merano, Rudolph Hruska, who had been involved with Dr. Porsche and Karl Rabe on the Volkswagen project from 1939 to 1941.

Ferry Porsche and Karl Rabe were unable to travel outside Germany or Austria at that time due to postwar restrictions, and Ferdinand Porsche and Louise's husband Anton were still in prison because of "war crimes." Ferry Porsche suggested that Abarth and Hruska, who were both free to travel, might like to act as Porsche's agents to sell the company's design services in Italy.

Hruska and Abarth had other things on their minds, though, and, at the instigation of Tazio Nuvolari and with the assistance of Corrado Millanta and Johnny Lurani, approached Porsche to design a new Grand Prix car to be built in Italy under Porsche supervision. Porsche agreed to do it, and backing for the project was obtained from Piero Dusio, owner of the Cisitalia company in Torino.

Porsche subsequently entered into an agreement to design a Grand Prix car, a small tractor, a sports car and a water turbine for Cisitalia. Part of the money (1,000,000 French francs) advanced for the work was turned over to the French authorities to get Dr. Porsche and Anton Piech out of prison. This was accomplished on August 1, 1947.

A visit by Ferry Porsche and Karl Rabe to Torino in mid-1947 (one of their first trips outside Germany after the war) was to see the progress being made on the Type 360—the Cisitalia GP car. This visit proved to be a pivotal point in Porsche history. What interested Porsche and Rabe even more than the Grand Prix car was the fact that Dusio had not gone ahead with the Porsche-designed sports car because he was having so much success with his Fiat-based cars.

The Cisitalia coupes and cabriolets, with their beautiful Pinin Farina bodywork were light, and fast, but expensive to build because of their hand-built tubular space frames. Despite this, Dusio had plans to build 500 cars—coupes and convertibles—which were to sell for $5,000 in Italy, and $7,000 in export markets. This was a tremendous price for a car with a Fiat 1100 engine, transmission and rear axle; no matter how good-looking it was.

When Porsche and Rabe returned to their offices in Gmünd, they immediately revived a previously conceived plan for a Porsche-designed, Porsche-built sports car, with the design number 356.

Unlike Dusio's expensive and time-consuming method of building cars, they wanted a car based on a production chassis and running gear. For this project they had chosen the Volkswagen, which not only served their purpose admirably, but also was the product of the elder Porsche's inventive mind more than a decade earlier.

In spite of their belief that a hand-built space frame was uneconomical for any sort of mass production, the first Porsche was built with inexpensive Volkswagen components—but held together by a space frame. The engine was in front of the rear axle; a position not to be duplicated by another Porsche until the 550 Spyder in 1953. Erwin Komenda designed a simple roadster body, fabricated from aluminum, to clothe the Volkswagen mechanical components. The car was driven to Switzerland in June 1948, and was the subject of tests by automotive

The first Porsche, as it looked when completed in Gmünd, Austria, in May 1948. It was a mid-engined car with an aluminum body designed by Erwin Komenda.

Porsche number 1; the matriarch—or patriarch, depending on your perspective—of all Porsches. The aluminum body covered a Volkswagen suspension and modified VW engine, held to-

gether by a space frame. Unlike future road-going Porsches, the engine was *ahead* of the rear axle. It has been recently restored by the factory. *Author*

15

journalists at the time of the Swiss Grand Prix at Bern on July 4.

On July 11, the roadster, driven by Prof. Porsche's nephew, Herbert Kaes, won a "round the houses" race in Innsbruck, Austria—the first-ever Porsche racing victory. Ferry Porsche, in the meantime, had been planning a car that would be more practical, both for manufacturing and sales, to replace the original car.

The new design, 356/2, placed the engine behind the rear axle as it had been in the Volkswagen. This simplified manufacture and allowed considerably more luggage space. The frame was built up from sheet steel into a platform with welded box-section side sills and a central "tunnel" which added chassis stiffness and provided a space for wiring and controls to run from the front to the back of the car. A coupe and cabriolet were planned.

Production of the Austrian-built 356/2 reached only four cars in 1948, twenty-five cars in 1949 and eighteen cars in 1950. The major problem was body construction, as they were built by hand in Gmünd. By spring of 1951, Porsche had sold only fifty-one cars of the 356/2 type; forty-three coupes and eight cabriolets—six of the latter were bodied by Beutler, in Switzerland, and the other two by Porsche, as were the coupes.

Volkswagen, meanwhile, was rising from the ashes of World War II, under the direction of Heinz Nordhoff and, in September 1948, Porsche became a design consultant to Volkswagenwerk. This arrangement benefited VW not only from the engineering side, but also effectively kept Porsche from working for a competing car company.

Members of the Porsche family had been wanting to move their operation back to Stuttgart, and reached this goal in two stages in 1950. First, they rented a bit more than 5,000 square feet of space in Reutter's body plant to perform final assembly of the cars, and soon afterward an 1,100-square-foot building was purchased to serve as office and design space.

It was on the day before Good Friday of 1950 when the first German-built Porsche made its debut, which was only one of several events that year which were of utmost importance to Porsche. Professor Porsche's seventy-fifth birthday was celebrated on September 3, and a month later Porsche's small exhibit of two cars at the Paris Auto Salon marked the fiftieth anniversary of the first Porsche-designed car's exhibit—the electric Lohner-Porsche—at the Universal Exposition in Paris in 1900.

Professor Porsche was stricken by a stroke in November 1950, and he succumbed to his illness on January 30, 1951.

Many automobile companies have started as family owned and operated businesses, but Porsche remains unique in that after forty-two years as a builder of fine cars, the company is still fifty percent family owned.

Because of sibling rivalry, and the fear of nepotism hurting the company, management was turned over to trusted employees in 1972, and the families became stockholders only. Ferry Porsche, his sister Louise Piech, and their eight children each held ten percent of the company. Since 1972, management had been by someone other than a Porsche or Piech family member. In 1984, a major change took place when one third of the company's capital stock was offered on the German stock exchange in the form of non-voting preferred shares. Then, one sixth of the company's stock was converted into non-voting preferred shares and made available to family members for additional liquidity at their discretion.

The bank had planned to take three days to sell the 420,000 shares offered, but the offering, with a DM 50 book value, which went out at DM 780 and quickly rose to 1,000, was sold out in three hours! It had been planned to limit individuals to 100 shares and institutions to 2,000 shares, but this was quickly reduced to 10 and 200 limits.

As this update is being written, in the fall of 1989, Porsche production for the 1990 models (for the U.S. market) includes: 944 S2 Coupe, $41,900; 944 S2 Cabriolet, $48,600; 911 Carrera 2 Coupe, $58,700; 911 Carrera 2 Targa, $60,100; 911 Carrera 2 Cabriolet, $67,000; 911 Carrera 4 Coupe, $69,500; 911 Carrera 4 Targa, $70,900; 911 Carrera 4 Cabriolet, $77,800; and 928 Coupe (automatic or five-speed), $74,545.

Anton Piech with the first Porsche coupe, completed in July 1948 in Gmünd, Austria. It was also the first rear-engined Porsche; the type 356/2. Also a Komenda design, the body was aluminum and it had opening quarter windows. The subsequent Gmünd-built coupes had curved plexiglass fixed quarter windows. *Werkfoto*

The 944 Turbo is still available in Germany, but is not made as a legal U.S. car. It could, probably, be made U.S. legal but this is an extremely costly procedure and, in the author's opinion, not advisable. Aside from the cost, U.S. emission and safety conversions seem to beg for legal, and dealer service, problems.

It is a superb balance of high-quality, high-performance machinery, albeit at a high price. Porsches are not for those drivers who simply want transportation from point A to point B, nor are they for those who don't appreciate what they're getting for their money. Unfortunately, there are Porsche buyers (as there are those who buy Ferrari, Mercedes-Benz, Lamborghini or Maserati) who bought the car because "it was the thing to do," in order to be "in" with the "in" crowd.

We can only feel sympathy for those buyers. They've spent a lot of money for the best that's available, but they don't know (nor maybe care) why. They would be better off driving something else, but their patronage of the marque does help keep Porsche in business to build cars for those who do know and care. Maybe we should be grateful that

"they" do buy Porsches—by increasing the total number sold, it could help keep the price from skyrocketing even higher.

Early VW engine with Porsche modifications was used in early Porsches. It produced 40 hp at a time when the stock VW unit had 25 hp. *Author*

17

★★★	Coupe, Cabriolet
★★★★	Speedster
★★★★★	Gmünd-built cars

356

Late in 1949, Porsche, then operating under the official name of "Dr.-Ing.h.c.F. Porsche KG," in Stuttgart-Zuffenhausen, ordered 500 bodies from Reutter Karozzerie. The bodies were to be delivered at the rate of eight or nine per month.

Based on reaction from potential dealers and customers, Porsche management believed that it could sell 500 cars of this design, but wasn't sure how long it might take.

Original projections were abandoned by mid-1950 as sales accelerated beyond Porsche's wildest dreams. Deliveries actually started in April 1950, and by the end of the year 298 cars had been built and sold—an average rate of thirty-three per month.

The "chassis" consisted of a boxed, pressed-steel assembly in unit with the floor pan, full independent suspension with parallel trailing arms on each side in front and swing-axle rear with the wheels located by a single, flexible trailing arm on each side. Transverse torsion bars (laminated into a square section in front, round at the rear) supplied the spring medium. The shock absorbers were hydraulic; tubular in front and lever-type at the rear. Brakes on the Gmünd-built cars were cable-operated mechanical units from the Volkswagen, but VW switched to hydraulic brakes in 1950, and these were incorporated into the Stuttgart-built Porsches.

The engine, at the back, was a Porsche-modified Volkswagen unit of 1,131 cubic centimeters displacement although many of the cars built at Gmünd during 1949 had 73.5 instead of 75 mm bores, which resulted in 1086 cc—allowing them to run in the 1100 cc competition classes. Either engine drove through a VW four-speed nonsynchromesh transmission. Two Solex 26 VFJ carburetors were used on the Gmünd cars, but Solex 32 PBI carburetors were used on the Stuttgart cars. Each engine was assembled by one workman who took twenty-five hours to do the job.

Flat glass was used for the side windows, and the two-piece vee windshield was flat from the center to the outer three to four inches which was curved.

Interiors were Spartan by any standards, and particularly so compared to today's Porsches. Some literature lists a bench seat as standard for the early 1949 Gmünd-built cars, with bucket seats optional (no rear seats were provided), but there is little evidence that many were built this way. A bench seat was later listed as an option on 356 A and B cars but, again, there can't be more than a handful built with that option.

1951

For 1951, the Porsche 356 remained visually almost the same as the 1950 model; but underneath, it got two leading-shoe Lockheed-type hydraulic brakes from Ate, and tubular shock absorbers replaced the lever-arm type at the rear during the model run.

A 1286 cc engine was added, by enlarging the bore to 80 mm. It produced 44 hp, four

Beutler, in Switzerland, built six of the eight Cabriolet bodies for the Gmünd 356/2 series cars. They had two-piece flat-glass vee windshields and full-wheel discs. The Porsche lettering was on the front lid, unlike later models which had it below the opening.

An aluminum frame around the license plate area and valances off to each side were designed for the Gmünd coupe, but fortunately left off later Porsches. The windshield wipers parked in the upright position for unknown reasons (this, too, was later changed). The first Gmünd-built coupe had two-piece vee windshields and flat plexiglass side windows with opening vent wings. Subsequent cars (this is number 17 built in 1949) had non-opening curved quarter windows in an early search for better aerodynamics. Curved windshields came later. *Author*

more than the 1100 engine, at 4200 rpm. In October, the 1488 cc engine became the top option, with roller-bearing rod journals and two Solex 40 PBIC carburetors. This engine was actually a 1952 model power plant.

Many myths surrounded the "roller-bearing engine" then, and still do. Low friction and high revs were the most commonly stated reasons for this expensive and complicated assembly. Generally speaking, the primary reasons for a roller-bearing rod journal are to obtain a one-piece connecting rod, which is inherently stronger than a two-piece rod, and to eliminate the necessity for high oil pressure at high rpm. Porsche's reason for adopting this design was simpler: According to Karl Ludvigsen in *Porsche: Excellence Was Expected*, the absence of rod bolts at the lower end allowed an increase of 5 mm on the crank throw radius, which resulted in a stroke increase of 10 mm. The longer stroke, of 74 mm, brought the engine displacement up to 1488 cc. All other considerations, according to Ludvigsen, were secondary.

The roller-bearing-crank engines acquired a reputation of fragility that was not entirely deserved. In the hands of customers who drove these cars on the road, the engine needed an expensive overhaul more often than a plain-bearing engine would have. But this type of engine installed in a racing car proved extremely reliable—probably because the engine was set up and maintained properly, and the car was driven in the manner for which it was intended. An engine with a roller-bearing crank did not respond kindly to lugging, and customers were admonished to "keep the revs up or you'll hammer the roller bearings flat." This was probably good advice as far as it went, but the philosophy rubbed off on the drivers of Porsches with plain-bearing engines, and the sound of Porsches on the streets in the early 1950s was always one of "two gears too low, and 2,000 revs too high."

1952

Important changes were made in 1952: A one-piece windshield was adopted (two flat sections, with a "fold" at the vertical center line); a folding rear seat was added; the spare wheel was moved farther to the front in a near-vertical position, allowing more luggage space; brake drum diameter was increased from 230 to 280 mm (from nine to eleven inches), width from 30 to 40 mm; and a fully-synchronized transmission with the patented Porsche split-ring synchromesh became standard on all models. Stronger bumpers were set out from the body.

At the suggestion of U.S. Porsche distributor Max Hoffman, a lightweight roadster—the America—was built. Of the sixteen Americas, fourteen came to the United States where most were raced successfully by private owners on both coasts.

Possibly the most significant, and lasting, change for 1952 was the creation of the Porsche emblem. Taken from a sketch drawn by Ferry Porsche on a napkin, while lunching with Max Hoffman, the final design was the work of Porsche publicity chief Lepper, and Porsche engineer Reimspiess.

This emblem, which is so well known today, is made of a background of the crest of the State of Baden-Wurttemburg, with its six staghorns. In the center is the coat of arms of Stuttgart—a rampant black horse on a yellow shield. The horse represents the old area of Stuttgart which had been a stud farm (Stuotgarten). Ferry Porsche has alluded to a historical tie between the prancing horse of Stuttgart and the prancing horse of Ferrari—both of which are black on a yellow shield.

1953

Visually, the 1953 Porsches were much like the late 1952s, but improvements were made in soundproofing and general equipment. In November a roller-bearing 1300S engine was introduced as a 1954 model.

1954

Six engines were offered during the 1954 model year—1100, 1300, 1300S, 1300A, 1500 and 1500S—but only the 1500 and 1500S were exported to the United States. American importer Max Hoffman didn't accept the smaller-displacement models for sale in the United States. He thought, and was probably right, that Americans wouldn't buy the smaller engine sizes at the price the cars would have to be sold for in the United States. Further, he made the 1500S his "top

The rear of the Gmünd-built coupe was about as barren of decoration as you'll find on a Porsche; the need for license-plate light, back-up light, bumper uprights and the mandatory reflectors came later. Even the bumper, though, was more for looks than it was for practical work. *Author*

Turn indicators, or "trafficators," as the British called them, were of the swing-arm type in the late forties. A light in the end went on when the arm was raised, day or night, and could be seen from both front and rear through the plastic sides of the arm. *Author*

A 160 km/h speedometer was set behind a "banjo" type steering wheel reminiscent of many late-thirties American cars (Ford and Buick come to mind). The interior was not as complete or as elegant as later Porsches, but the developing style was already evident. *Author*

21

of the line" and the 1500 America the standard model.

Aside from the engine differences, the lower-priced version had no radio, aluminum wheel trim rings, passenger's sun visor, adjustable passenger's seatback, or the fold-ing rear seatback—all of which were standard on the 1500 Super.

On March 15, 1954, the five-thousandth Porsche was driven off the line in Stuttgart—a production figure no one at Porsche would have dreamed possible four years ear-

By the end of 1950, the first Reutter-built Cabriolets appeared. The Reutter emblem on the side has been seen with a height-placement varia-tion of almost three inches. *Kurt Worner/Road & Track*

lier when they talked bravely of eight or nine cars per month.

The heater control was moved from the dashboard to the floor "tunnel" and a windshield washer became standard equipment. In September the Speedster was added to the line—for export to the United States only. Like the 1954 models, the Speedster was equipped with 406 mm (sixteen-inch) wheels until the 356A models were introduced in October 1955.

1955

Production started on the 1955 models in November 1954. Visual changes were minimal; a longer, crested hood handle was used and some models carried the name "Continental" on the side of the front fenders. The major changes were mechanical. Engines had a three-piece aluminum crankcase instead of the two-piece magnesium case as before, and had oil capacity of 4.5 liters compared to the previous 3.5 liters. Many of the engine's dimensions and the general layout were similar to the two-piece crankcase engine, but the new parts were not interchangeable with the old engine components. Porsche thus moved further away from dependency on Volkswagen parts.

Another significant change in November 1954 was the addition of a front anti-roll bar, which was accompanied by a change in front spring rate—the lower laminated bar retained its original five leaves, but the upper bar now had six.

Because of the availability of Speedster bodies, and the start of its own total engine production, Porsche production reached as many as twelve cars per day, and 2,952 Porsches—Coupe, Cabriolet and Speedster—were built during the 1955 model run. A new model, the 356 A, would be started in October 1955, as a 1956 model; but what were the 356s like?

Early driver reports, road impressions and road tests can give us a clue. In England's *Light Car* of September 1951, it was reported that "If the steering has a 'different' feel at cruising speeds of 70 mph it is completely accurate, high-geared, light and free from wander. The comfort of one's ride over all types of surface is one of the delights of the car. Pot-holed roads, adverse cambers, hump-

backed bridges, can all be taken with confidence at a fast cruising speed."

And, the writer continued, "The Porsche engine . . . is mounted behind the rear axle, a position which creates marked oversteer characteristics. This is by no means a fault of design but is something which the new owner must learn before the combination of wet road and over-enthusiastic right foot induces the Dreaded Spin."

These last words were repeated many times in many ways during the lifetime of the 356 models.

John Bentley, writing in the January 1952 edition of *Auto* (Petersen Publishing Company), said: ". . . the first things that impressed me were the high grade detail workmanship and the amazing amount of front seat room," and "Steering is so light that despite its fairly high gearing I got the deceptive impression of steering wheel 'play' when in fact, there is none . . . Steering response is

Pre-1952 Porsche 356 models had the spare tire mounted almost horizontally in the front compartment, leaving little space for anything but the gas tank and windshield washer fluid reservoir just behind the tire. *Road & Track*

so quick that I had to accustom myself to 'wishing' the car through turns, the slightest wheel movement being enough when used in conjunction with the throttle."

Further into the report, Bentley wrote: "Should the sporting purist take the car out for the sheer fun of driving, mastery of the gearbox offers a stimulating challenge rewarded by a sense of achievement . . . In the near future the Porsche will be coming out with synchromesh and one serious criticism of this outstanding car will be eliminated."

The writer was right on target with his remarks about space, handling and the as-yet nonsynchromesh transmission, but his conclusion to the article was a bit faulty, in retrospect: "Porsche production is rising toward 100 cars a month, but is unlikely ever to exceed this figure, no matter how great the backlog of orders." Well, John, you can't win 'em all.

A year later in the January 1953 issue of *Auto*, Dick van Osten wrote: "This is not the type of car that Mr. Average Man can hurl around the first time he steps behind the wheel. The Porsche requires a different technique that is alien to most of us; but, once mastered, the car will do your bidding with an absolute minimum of effort. The basic key to success in handling a Porsche is to use about half the effort you usually use in driving." Commenting of the mechanical design, van Osten said, "The argument of front *vs.* rear engine location will go on forever, but here is some food for thought. Dr. Porsche once said that it does not make any difference where the engine is located as long as it is light. The Porsche engine weighs 160 lbs!"

In the March 1953 *Autosport*, John Gott was impressed with the performance of the new Porsches: "The Tulip Rally, in which Ray Brookes and I drove my 1947 H.R.G., gave me a chance to meet the Porsches in direct competition for the first time. Nine Porsches started in the 1500cc sports class . . . On the run from Brussels to Rheims, whilst cruising at around 75 m.p.h., I was startled to be passed by a Porsche which had left Brussels 28 minutes behind me. However, I was not therefore unduly shocked when Porsches took eight of the 10 class placings on the timed climb on the Ballon d'Alsace."

Later in his report, Gott commented: "I counted myself extremely lucky to finish fourth at Zandvoort, behind Van der Lof and Porsches of Van der Muhle and Nathan, and certainly would not have done this had not three Porsches displayed a defect in road holding and crashed into the sand dunes. Observing these unpleasing sights from the immediate rear, I came to the conclusion that when driven into corners at the extreme high speeds of which the cars are capable, the combination of swing axle, rear mounted engine and low general weight caused a breakaway at racing speeds to come without warning and some violence."

After the Liege-Rome-Liege rally, writer/competitor Gott had more observations about the Porsches: "The 'works' drivers stressed that not only was competition found to be the best test bed, but that the successes gained in competitions all over the world were invaluable publicity."

A different observation of the early Porsches came from Maurice Gatsonides, writing in the June 5, 1953, *Autosport*: "The lights, possibly adequate for other types, are certainly not strong enough for the speeds possible with the Super."

The British magazine *The Autocar* tested a 1954 Porsche coupe for the November 1953 edition and was exceedingly charitable in its report of a non-British design, saying, among other things: "The gear change, operated by a short, slender central lever with a large knob, is one of the most pleasant and certainly one of the fastest manually operated changes experienced. It is possible to make noiseless changes just as fast as the driver can move the lever." And, "The brakes are in keeping with the performance, the car pulling up straight even with all wheels locked. The pedal pressure required for an emergency stop is fairly heavy, but at no time was any tendency to fade noticed."

All magazines which reported on the early Porsches were in general agreement on all aspects of the cars; excellent quality, lack of wind noise, superb synchromesh transmission (after the development of the Porsche synchromesh system), abundant space for large drivers, excellent brakes and superior handling—for an expert or skilled driver.

But, in the hands of an incautious, inexperienced or less-than-skillful driver, the car could be treacherous.

A thinking Porsche salesman would warn his customers that a few months and several thousand miles of experience should be gained before playing "boy racer"; particularly on a back country road with curves, some of which might be off-camber, or have drop-offs. A 356 Porsche could be driven

In 1950, production started in Stuttgart and the cars acquired windshields with the ends rounded for better airflow to the body sides. The bodies were made by Reutter (note the unusual Reutter emblem on the side). *Kurt Worner/Road & Track*

Stuttgart-built coupe of 1950 had the form that would continue through the 1955 model year; steel body by Reutter, with two-piece windshield (flat in the center and curved at the outer edges), two round and two rectangular lights

flanking the light bar over the rear plate and a single round parking/turn-signal lens under each headlight. The Porsche lettering was now standardized in design and mounted front and rear under the opening lids. *Author*

25

exceedingly fast—if the driver had the right feel for the car, but it could also get a driver into trouble faster than almost anything on the road if the driver was over his head. A tail-heavy car with swing-axle independent rear suspension is not forgiving, and is quick to let the less-than-prudent driver know that he has gone beyond his limit.

Several removable hardtops were available for the Speedster. Glasspar made one, illustrated, of fiberglass, and the factory also offered one in fiberglass. *Ralph Poole*

A 1955 Speedster with the stock top; a device that looked awful, kept some of the rain off, and seemed to make no difference to the cars' owners who loved the "inverted bathtub." *Ralph Poole/Author*

Unlike the thin Speedster top, the Cabriolet top was padded, which gave it a smoother look and made the interior quieter. With its roll-up windows, the Porsche Cabrio was one of the most weather-proof of convertibles.

The 1955 Speedster interior displayed the functionally stark design. The Cabriolet and Coupe still had the "bent in the center" flat vee windshield with curved outer edges but the Speedster had a fully curved windshield—a style that would be adopted by all Porsche models late in the year when the 356A was announced. *Ralph Poole*

A 1955 356 Cabriolet with similar dash to the Continental, but different detailing. This radio is a Telefunken. A special floor mat has been fitted over the stock rubber mat.

A 1955 356 Continental Coupe interior. Fuel reserve handle and fuel filter were under dash. The radio is an aftermarket unit made by Motorola. *Author*

Side by side comparison of a 1955 Continental Coupe and Speedster shows the similarity in body design, but difference in windshields. The striper's brush has, unfortunately, been applied to the Coupe. Porsche dropped the Continental name in 1956, in deference to Lincoln when it brought out the Continental Mark II. *Ralph Poole*

356 (1950–55)

Engine

Design: .... Air-cooled flat (opposed) four
Type: 1100 (April 1950–mid-1954) ..... 369, 2-piece crankcase, plain-bearing crank
1300 (Jan 1951–May 1955) .... 506, 2-piece crankcase, plain-bearing crank
1500 (Oct 1951–Sept 1952) .... 527, 2-piece crankcase, roller-bearing crank
1500 (Sept 1952–Nov 1954) .... 546, 2-piece crankcase, plain-bearing crank
1500S (Oct 1952–Nov 1954) .... 528, 2-piece crankcase, roller-bearing crank
1300S (Nov 1953–May 1954) .... 589, 2-piece crankcase, roller-bearing crank
1300A (June 1954–Nov 1954) ..... 506/1, 2-piece crankcase, plain-bearing crank
1300 (Nov 1954–Oct 1955) .... 506/2, 3-piece crankcase, plain-bearing crank
1300S (Nov 1954–Oct 1955) .... 589/2, 3-piece crankcase, roller-bearing crank
1500 (Nov 1954–Oct 1955) .... 546/2, 3-piece crankcase, plain-bearing crank
1500S (Nov 1954–Oct 1955) ...... 528/2, 3-piece crankcase, roller-bearing crank
Borexstroke, mm/inches: 1100 .... 73.5x64/2.89x2.52
1300 (Jan 1951–May 1954) 80x64/3.15x2.52
1300S, 1300A 74.5x74/2.93x2.91
1500, 1500S 80x74/3.15x2.91
1300 (Nov 1954–Oct 1955) 74.5x74/2.93x2.91
Displacement, cc/cubic inches: 1100 .... 1086/66.7
1300 .... 1286/78.4
1300S, 1300A (1300 Nov 1954–Oct 1955) 1290/78.7
1500, 1500S 1488/90.6
Valve operation: .... Single camshaft with pushrods & rocker arms; inclined exhaust valves
Compression ratio: 1100, 1500 .... 7:1
1300, 1300A 6.5:1
1300S, 1500S 8.2:1

Carburetion: 1100, 1300, 1300S, 1300A, 1500 .... Two Solex 32 PBI
1300S (1955–56) .... Two Solex 32 PBIC or 40 PICB
1500S (till Nov 1954) .... Two Solex 40 PBIC
1500S (Nov 1954–Oct 1955) .... Two Solex 40 PICB
BHP (Mfr): 1100 .... 40 DIN/46 SAE @ 4200
1300, 1300A .... 44 DIN/50 SAE @ 4200
1500 (Oct 1951–Sept 1952) .... 60 DIN/70 SAE @ 5000
1500 (Sept 1952–Nov 1954) .... 55 DIN/64 SAE @ 4400
1300S .... 60 DIN/70 SAE @ 5500
1500S .... 70 DIN/82 SAE @ 5000

Chassis & drivetrain

Frame: ...... Boxed-section pressed steel in unit with floor pan
Component layout: .... Rear engine, rear drive
Clutch: .... Fichtel & Sachs single dry-plate
Transmission: 1100 (through 1952) .... VW four-speed (all gears indirect)
1300 (through 1951) ...... VW four-speed (all gears indirect)
1100 (1953–1954) ...... Porsche four-speed, all-synchromesh (all gears indirect)
All others .... Porsche four-speed, all-synchromesh (all gears indirect)
Axle ratio: 4.43:1
Rear suspension: ..... Independent (swing axle) with transverse torsion bars & lever-action shock absorbers (changed to telescopic during 1951 model run)
Front suspension: ..... Independent, with parallel trailing arms, transverse laminated torsion bars, telescopic shock absorbers (anti-roll bar added in 1954)

General

Wheelbase, mm/inches: 2100/82.7
Track, front, mm/inches: 1290/50.8
rear, mm/inches: 1250/49.2
Brakes: 1100 (first cars) .... Mechanical, drum-type
All others .... Hydraulic, drum-type
Tire size, front & rear: 5.00–16
Wheels: .... Bolt-on, steel disc
Body builder: ...... Reutter (1952 America roadsters were built by Glaser, and some Cabriolets in 1950, '51 & '52 were built by Heuer)

The Coupe style lent itself to a rear-engined design because it easily covered the vertical fan, but the Speedster and Cabriolet required more "hump" in the back than might otherwise be used for a notchback design. *Ralph Poole*

Extras—factory or aftermarket—have always been popular with Porsche owners. This 1955 Continental has a luggage rack attached to the air intake grille (no self-respecting Porsche owner would drill holes in the body to attach one), chrome wheels and an Abarth exhaust system. *Ralph Poole*

29

Speedsters were often referred to as "inverted bathtubs" or "upside-down soap dishes" but were loved by their owners. The top was not one of its strong points; it not only looked ugly, but didn't shed water too well. In spite of the verbal jibes and leaky tops, the body style is now one of the most coveted, and has been duplicated in fiberglass for kit builders. *Ralph Poole*

This 1955 Continental Coupe is a two-owner car and, except for 15-inch wheels, is original in all respects. The car was purchased first just after the Los Angeles auto show in October 1954. Unless the car is to be entered in concours where authenticity is a prime factor, I think the change to 15-inch wheels was a smart move because better tires in more sizes are available, and the handling was improved with the wider tire contact patch. *Author*

Chapter 3

356A

Production of the first 356A, a 1956 model, started in October 1955. Five engines were offered: 1300, 1300S, 1600, 1600S and 1500GS. Only the latter three were exported to America. The car looked little different, but it had a new windshield and dash, and significant suspension modifications.

The engines were still air-cooled flat-fours, and all but the 1500GS Carrera were the standard Porsche pushrod-and-rocker-arm ohv design. The 1500GS engine was a detuned version of the four-cam (double overhead on each bank) 550 Spyder engine introduced in 1954. The Carrera engine had a Hirth roller-bearing crankshaft (rollers on both mains and rods), 8.7:1 compression ratio, dry-sump lubrication and produced 100 DIN horsepower at 6200 rpm.

All 356A engines had warm air directed from the cylinders to the carburetors for quicker warm-up. This air supply was thermostatically controlled by a bellows near the fan housing. Catering to a broader spectrum of customers, the flywheel was made heavier—to smooth out the idle, and to allow smoother starts. The carburetor linkage was also changed.

A new transmission, the Type 644, was used. This unit had a one-piece housing (previous gearboxes were split along the centerline) with the gear shafts installed through the front. At the same time, the front transmission mounting was changed from a single rubber pad to twin circular rubber mounts.

Suspension had been "softened" at the front by eliminating leaves from the laminated torsion bars, and now at the rear by lengthening the torsion bars from 21.8 to 24.7 inches, and reducing the bar diameter from 25 to 24 mm.

Wheels of the 356A were of fifteen-inch diameter with 4.5-inch-wide rims, compared to the sixteen-inch by 3.25 rims of the 356.

Body styles for the 1956 356A were Coupe, Cabriolet and Speedster; each available with all engine options (1300 not available in Speedster). All three body types were built by Reutter, in Stuttgart. The windshield was now a one-piece curved glass unit, and the dash was padded and upholstered in either leather or imitation leather. Both front seats were fully reclining, and the rear seatbacks could be folded down to carry more luggage.

A new instrument panel carried three large, round instrument dials: speedometer, tachometer and combined fuel level and oil temperature gauges. Headlight flashers were now standard equipment—except on Speedsters.

1957

Body design remained unchanged from 1956, but minor cosmetic changes were made in the spring of 1957: Padded sun visors became standard, the speedometer was moved from the left to the right side of the panel, and the dial for the fuel/oil temperature gauge was moved to the left. Outside, "teardrop" taillights (mounted hori-

A 1956 Porsche 356A 1600 Super, equipped for German delivery. The chrome-plated wheels and center-lock hubs were optional equipment. The hub nuts had no "wings" or "ears" because of German restrictions on projections that could harm pedestrians. Projecting radiator ornaments (which wouldn't affect Porsche) were outlawed at the same time. *Author.*

The 1956 356A Speedster panel; stark but functional. Instruments included: center, 6000 rpm tach; left, 120 mph speedometer; right, fuel level and oil temperature gauges.

zontally) replaced the twin round lights of previous models, and the license plate/back-up light bar was moved from above the plate to a position below the license plate.

Several running changes were made to the engine during 1957: Offset piston wrist pins were adapted to the 1600 engine to counteract piston "slap" in a cold engine (inherent with air-cooled engines), and the normal 356 engines were given the aluminum camshaft gear, which was already used on the 1600 Super, to replace the fiber-toothed gear.

1958

The 1958 Porsche 356A, again, was visually like its predecessors—to the uninitiated. While retaining the basic shape, the T-2 body (an internal Porsche designation of the 1958 models) had vent wings in the door glass of the Cabriolet (the Coupe also had wind wings, but mounted on the door frame, outside the window); the exhaust pipe tips were in the lower part of the vertical bumper guards for a higher departure angle (better clearance for steep driveways but also got the bumpers dirty); the Speedster and Cabriolet had larger rear windows, and a removable hardtop was available for the Cabriolet as a factory option. An aftermarket fiberglass top had been made by Glasspar in Newport Beach, California, for the Speedster. A factory fiberglass hardtop was made by Brendel.

Under the skin, more changes were made: Cast-iron cylinders were used in the 1600 Normal engine, which was standard practice for Volkswagen but the first for Porsche since the early 356 1100. The results, for this primarily touring car, were lower manufacturing cost and a quieter engine, with only minimal weight increase.

The 1300 engine was dropped, all Porsche pushrod engines ran in plain bearings (the Carrera and Spyder four-cam engines retained the roller-bearing cranks), the carburetors were now Zenith NDIX assemblies, and the Fichtel & Sachs coil-spring clutch was replaced by the Haussermann diaphragm spring unit.

A new steering box, a Ross-type worm-and-stud design made by ZF, replaced the VW worm-and-nut steering design. The steering ratio increased from 14.15:1 to 16:1. At the same time, a larger—16¾-inch diameter—steering wheel (already used on the Carreras) became standard on all Porsches, further reducing steering effort because of better leverage.

1959

Porsche got an early start on 1959 when a replacement for the Speedster went into production in August 1958. This car, initially called the Speedster D, had a higher windshield with a chrome frame, and a top that was between the low, blind Spartan design of the Speedster, and the padded deluxe top of the Cabriolet. The body retained the side chrome strip of the Speedster, and had some of the visual character of the Speedster, but was considerably more practical and comfortable. These bodies were built by Drauz, from which came the "D" and before the public introduction, the car became the "Convertible D." The Coupe and Cabriolet, built by Reutter, continued as before.

Late in 1958, single, progressively wound valve springs replaced the dual springs in all Porsche pushrod engines.

Production of the 356A ended in September 1959, when the 356B was introduced.

Going back to magazine road tests and owner comments, we can find out what was thought of the "A" model.

One of the first road reports on the 356A appeared in the November 18, 1955, issue of *The Autocar*, and the writer caught the spirit of the car just as I imagine the designers had planned it: "Thus we find the 1956 Porsche almost in a class by itself for the combination it offers of high cruising and maximum speeds without mechanical fuss, coupled with real economy in fuel consumption and, for a sporting vehicle, excellent comfort for two." Later in the same article, the writer commented on the displacement increase to 1582 cc: "The effect of this has been to improve the low speed torque characteristics, so that the Porsche is a little more tractable and less dependent on the gear lever; at the same time it possesses an increased ability to maintain speed on its very high top gear when confronted with a long gradient." And, this: ". . . to drive a Porsche is to experience a new form of motoring, so re-

This 1957 1600 engine has the Solex carburetors which were added in mid-year to replace
the twin Zeniths. *Ralph Poole*

Even with the spare tire mounted more vertically
in the front, the huge square gas tank kept the
useable space to a minimum. Most Porsche trav-
elers utilized the space behind the front seats
for larger luggage pieces, putting things they
wanted to hide in the front. *Ralph Poole*

This 356A 1600 has the standard one-piece
front bumper "bow" connected to the tall uprights, and what looks like aftermarket trim
rings on the wheels. The car in all three photos
on this page had been photographed for a 1957
Road & Track test report. *Ralph Poole*

freshingly different is it from the usual run of vehicles."

Across London, in the offices of *The Motor*, Joseph Lowrey wrote in the January 18, 1956, edition: "Having quite a personal liking for cars which can be 'wished' around corners without appreciable physical 'steering,' my first reaction was to prefer the handling of the 1955 car to the slightly more 'Americanized' controls of the 1956 model." Lowrey later in the same piece said: "I soon forgot my reactionary ideas."

Continuing, Lowrey dwelt on the greater flexibility of the new 1600 engine compared to the previous 1500, and hit upon a significant point with this observation: "My impression, incidentally, was that it was not really the engine which was in any way inflexible, but that the use of a short and 'solid' transmission line was probably making the use of low r.p.m. a jerky business. A spring centre clutch, long propeller shaft and axle mounted on 'cart' springs together provide flexibility which if cleverly used can reduce the 'resonant' speed of a transmission to a very low figure." This latter was in reference to front-engined cars with rear drive being generally less critical of engine rpm for driving smoothness.

In a full-scale road test of the 1600, *The Autocar* writer said, in the May 4, 1956, issue: "...the handling has less 'rear engine feel' to it." And, later, "... these cobbled downhill curves can be negotiated with an absolute stability that flatters any driver who has a light touch." Not all comments were laudatory in the report, for the driver noted: "When a window is open, discomfort is caused at high speed by reverberation of the air in the car which hurts the ears; because it is desirable to keep the window closed, some improvement in ventilation in warm weather is desirable."

Motor Trend editor Walt Woron, and writer Bob Rolofson, commented favorably about putting the Cabriolet or Speedster tops up and down, saying that even without power assist they were "one man" tops. The heavily-padded Cabriolet top made the car as quiet as the Coupe, and the Speedster top was claustrophobic. They were impressed with the quality—from overall fit and finish to the "... magnificent adjustable seats."

In 1958, when the hardtop became available, *Sports Cars Illustrated* (now *Car and Driver*) drove one in Europe. The writer liked the vision ("Rearward vision is better than in the Coupe") and the ventilation ("Ventilation in the hardtop is improved by two wind wings—optional on coupes and Cabriolets but standard here."); but didn't like other aspects of the removable hardtop: "When cracked open to allow the heater-ventilation system to operate efficiently, the wind noise is considerably louder than with the regular coupe's trailing quarter windows." The magazine staffers also liked the steering, saying: "The latest Porsche steering is a real improvement over the first 356As. Considerably lighter and with quicker return, we found the Ross box to be most satisfactory." The steering was a Ross design, but was made by ZF.

The Autocar, October 10, 1958, carried a test report on the Porsche 1600 "Damen," a nickname given to the most docile of the 1958 356As, and waxed eloquent about the car: "As soon as one moves off from rest, it is clear that the Porsche's individual character is not confined to its design alone. One quickly begins to feel a part of it—as though one were wearing, rather than sitting in the car. Acceleration is impressive, particularly so because of the seemingly effortless way in which the car gathers speed, the almost complete absence of transmission noise, and the low level of road induced body noise." And, later: "Somehow the car seems to slip through traffic, eagerly taking advantage of every gap that presents itself; the impressive performance in first and second in part accounts for this."

Perhaps John Jerome explained the Porsche owner's philosophy best. Writing in the September 1967 *Car and Driver* about his own 356A Speedster, John said: "The car oversteered like crazy until you started fiddling with it. Clutch cables broke occasionally, clutches burned out regularly and throttle linkages fell off often (at any one of at least 12 different connection points that I can remember offhand). The oil radiator, hidden inside the fan shrouding, would sometimes develop copious leaks, and it was easier but messier to keep adding oil than to tear the engine apart to get to the oil cooler.... You

Early 1957 Coupe, left, shows the light above the plate, one-piece upper bumper bow, moon caps and four taillights. *Ralph Poole.* The late

1957, right, has light below plate, two-piece upper bumper, teardrop taillights and crested, protruding hubcaps.

Other than the steering wheel, this early 1957 Speedster interior is very much like the 1956 model. *Author*

This early 1957 Speedster has the heater control behind the shift lever, which was standard for that time. In mid-model run positions were switched—shift lever behind the heater control. *Author*

Both the similarities and the differences between this 1959 Convertible D and the 1957 Speedster, opposite page, can be seen; the bodies and trim are identical, but the Convertible D top is higher and includes roll-up windows. *Ralph Poole*

Speedster seats (these are early 1957) were simple buckets with little padding, which were both comfortable and supportive for fast driving. *Author*

overlooked those things. You liked the way the doors and hinges worked. You liked the way the car was so all-of-a-piece that nothing ever rattled. You liked the screwball handling, so easy to dirt-track around . . . and so capable of convincing you that you were really pretty fast after all."

The oversteer characteristics of the 356s could be alleviated somewhat by decambering the rear wheels (but don't carry as much load if the rear is decambered or you'll "bottom out" on dips in the road), and by carrying more pressure—five to seven pounds higher—in the rear tires than in the front.

And so it went. Magazine writers in Europe, England and the United States all found a little to complain about when reviewing the 356A—wind noise with the vent wings open, lack of out-of-sight baggage space, the tail-heavy weight distribution coupled with swing-axle rear suspension

Speedsters, like this early 1957 1600 Super with chromed wheels and hubcaps, looked better with the tops down. Early 1957 models had the "moon" hubcaps, and high bumper uprights that helped protect the delicate Porsche bodies. All Speedsters had the thin chrome strip along the body side in line with the door handle, except GS/GT, four-cams and pushrod 1959s.

All 356 and 356A Porsches had the "five-bolt" door striker-plates set high on the door jamb until mid-1957, as shown on this early 1957 Speedster, left. In mid-1957, the striker-plate was moved to the center of the door jamb and remained this way through the B and C series 356 as shown on this 1959 1600 Coupe, right. At the same time, the shift lever and heater control switched places, the four round taillights were replaced by two teardrop units, the hubcaps became the protruding-center type with the Porsche crest, and the rear upper bumper bow became a two-piece unit. The rear lights, bumpers and hubcaps are often changed by Porsche owners, but the striker-plate and heater control/shift lever locations are excellent clues as to whether the car was built earlier or later than mid-1957. *Author*

that meant drivers had to be doubly careful at high speeds on curving roads.

On the whole, however, praise for the Porsche's quality was abundant in all aspects; the superior performance (seldom qualified by reference to engine size) in terms of both speed and economy, its excellent road-holding and, mainly, the sheer joy of driving such a responsive, eager car were the recurring themes prevalent in automotive magazine articles.

Although basically the same car as the first 356s, the 356A did have better brakes, better steering, better suspension and a better engine than its immediate predecessor.

The 356A Normal came equipped with the moon-type hubcaps, while the 1600S and Carrera GS had the deluxe caps, which proved popular enough that they started to appear on many other Porsche models—either ordered when new, or added later. *Author*

Square-end door handles, as on this 1955 Continental Coupe (top), were used until mid–1957, when they were changed to the somewhat more rounded design as on this 1959 1600 Coupe (bottom). *Author*

356A (1956–59)

Engine

Design: .... Air-cooled flat (opposed) four
Type: 1300 .... (Oct 1955–Sept 1957) 506/2, 3-piece crankcase, plain-bearing crank
1300S .... (Oct 1955–Sept 1957) 589/2, 3-piece crankcase,
roller-bearing crank
1600 .... (Oct 1955–Sept 1959) 616/1, 3-piece crankcase,
plain-bearing crank
1600S .... (Oct 1955–Sept 1957) 616/2, 3-piece crankcase,
roller-bearing crank
1600S .... (Oct 1957–Sept 1959) 616/2, 3-piece crankcase,
plain-bearing crank
Borexstroke, mm/inches: 1300, 1300S 74.5x74/2.93x2.91
1600, 1600S 82.5x74/3.25x2.91
Displacement, cc/cubic inches: 1300, 1300S 1290/78.7
1600, 1600S 1582/96.5
Valve operation: .... Single camshaft with pushrods & rocker
arms; inclined exhaust valves
Compression ratio: 1300 .... 6.5:1
1300S 8.2:1
1600 .... 7.5:1
1600S 8.5:1
Carburetion: 1300 .... Two Solex 32 PBI
1300S .... Two Solex 32 PBIC or 40 PICB
1600 .... 1958–59: Two Zenith NDIX, 1956–57: Two Solex 32
PBIC
1600S ..... 1956–57: Two Solex 40 PICB, 1958–59: Two Zenith
32 NDIX
BHP (Mfr): 1300 .... 44 DIN/50 SAE @ 4200
1300S .... 60 DIN/71 SAE @ 5500
1600 .... 60 DIN/70 SAE @ 4500
1600S .... 75 DIN/88 SAE @ 5000

Chassis & drivetrain

Frame: ...... Boxed-section pressed steel in unit with floor pan
Component layout: .... Rear engine, rear drive
Clutch: .... 1956–57: Fichtel & Sachs single dry-plate, 1958–
59: Haussermann single dry-plate
Transmission: .... Porsche four-speed, all-synchromesh (all
gears indirect)
Axle ratio: 4.43:1
Rear suspension: .... Independent (swing axle) with trans-
verse torsion bars & telescopic shock absorbers
Front suspension: .... Independent, with parallel trailing
arms, transverse laminated torsion bars, telescopic shock
absorbers & anti-roll bar

General

Wheelbase, mm/inches: 2100/82.7
Track, front, mm/inches: 1306/51.4
rear, mm/inches: 1372/50.1
Brakes: .... Aluminum drums with iron liners
Tire size, front & rear: 5.60–15
Wheels: .... Bolt-on steel disc
Body builder: .... Reuter (Coupe, Cabriolet, Speedster),
Convertible D (1959) Drauz

Early 1957 356A Porsches had the speedometer on the left, as on this 1600 Coupe (top), but later in the year the speedometer was on the right, as seen in this European delivery Cabriolet with a 200 km/h speedometer (bottom). Both cars have the standard rubber floor mats and carpeted kick panels. *Coupe photo, Ralph Poole; Cabriolet photo, Zwietason*

A 1958 356A 1600 European delivery model, with no upper bumper bows. The wire screen over the headlights was an optional item used originally by rallyists, to protect the lens from gravel thrown up by other cars, but adopted by enthusiast drivers as an indication of serious intentions. *Author*

A 1958 356A 1600 Super engine. Zenith carburetors used the same wire-mesh air filters as T–1 Supers with 40 mm single-throat Solexes. Zenith-carbed T–5 and T–6 Bs and Cs used can-type filters with paper elements. *Ralph Poole*

The side view of the 1958 Speedster is almost identical to the 1957, but this one has the louvered trim rings around the hubcaps. The dash looks much like the 1956, and 1957; but this one has a radio installed in front of the passenger and the steering wheel is a rare non-standard wheel. The rear looks much like a late 1957, with the low license-plate light, teardrop taillights and two-piece upper bumper bar; but the exhaust through the lower part of the bumper uprights indicates it is a 1958. *Ralph Poole*

A 1958 1600 Normal Cabriolet had the T-2 body, with its standard quarter windows and larger rear window. *Porsche Werkfoto*

A 1959 356A 1600 Coupe with all the extras, including an accessory luggage rack for the rear deck. The grille on the engine lid is for air intake, so the luggage doesn't get as much heat as one might expect from this location, but it does add weight in the wrong place: high and behind the rear axle. *Author*

The 1959 356A Convertible D had the side trim of the Speedster, and a top that was high like the Cabriolet but unpadded, like the Speedster. The top design of the Convertible D gave about as good visibility as was possible with a soft top. This car is one I tested, and reported on, in April 1959 *Road & Track. Ralph Poole*

The 1959 Convertible D, with body by Drauz, was a continuation of the Speedster but with roll-up windows, higher top, coupe seats and more luxurious trim. *Ralph Poole*

The 1959 Coupes, this one a 356A 1600, didn't have vent wings built into the door, but had a factory option pivoting wind wing on the outside. *Author*

The front bumper "bow" was raised during the 1959 model run to give a bit more protection.

The Convertible D, left, is an early '59; the Coupe, right, is a late 1959. *Ralph Poole/Author*

Interior of the 1959 356A 1600. A clock has been added to the center of the dash above the radio, the fuel reserve control can be seen just under the dash at right, the radio speakers mounted in the carpeted kick panels. The windshield washer was activated by the left foot (above brake and clutch pedals). *Author*

Detail of the 1959 356A parking light and air inlet to the front brake. *Author*

The 1959 1600 Coupe interior was superbly finished and, while very comfortable up front, was a bit tight in the back. The rear seat back folded flat to allow luggage to be placed on top—a necessary addition if traveling for any length of time where many changes of clothes were needed. *Author*

The serial number (107819) on the Reutter Karosserie plate identifies the car as a 1959 356A/1600 Coupe with a Type 616/1, three-piece crankcase engine with two 32 NDIX Solex carburetors. The engine bore and stroke are 82.5x74 and with a 7.5:1 compression ratio the engine delivers 60 DIN hp at 4500 rpm. *Author*

★★★

Chapter 4

356B

The most radical looking Porsche yet—the 1960 356B—made its public debut at the Frankfurt auto show in September 1959. The bumpers on this, the T–5, body were raised—3¾ inches in front, 4⅛ inches at the rear—to increase traffic and parking protection. Large, vertical bumper guards also helped in this respect. The headlights were raised so that the fender line went almost straight forward to the top edge of the chromed light frame. The parking lights protruded forward above the bumper, at the outboard edge of small twin grilles covering the horns. Air intakes, for brake cooling, were cut into the body on either side below the bumper.

Inside, the rear seats were lowered for more passenger head room, and the rear seatbacks were split so three persons and some luggage could be carried; or two, and more luggage. The rear window could be defrosted from outlets below the window. Ventilation was aided by vent wings in the door glass, which were standard on all bodies except the Roadster.

Brake drums with circumferential fins were replaced by new cast-aluminum drums with seventy-two radial fins; the cast-iron liners being held in place by the Alfin process. At the same time, a new seal was incorporated into the design, between the edge of the drum and the backing plate, to help keep water out of the brakes.

Engines were almost unchanged from the last 356A, but the 1600 Super 90 engine announced at Frankfurt didn't appear in production until March 1960. A number of crankshaft failures in early 356Bs caused Porsche engineers to enlarge oil pump capacity (by lengthening the gears), and the new pump was fitted to all 616 engines during the 1960 model run. Stronger rods and larger main bearing journals became standard on the Super 90.

The Type 741 transaxle had a single front mount, similar to the last 356. And, as before, Porsche engineers decided the double mount of the 356A was better, so after 3,000 of the 356Bs were built, they went back to the Type 644 design.

1961

Dutch-made Koni shock absorbers were fitted as standard equipment on both the 1600S and Super 90. Simultaneously, the rear roll stiffness was reduced by the use of one-millimeter-smaller torsion bars (24 to 23 mm). The addition of a transverse leaf spring helped carry the weight of the rear of the car, but didn't affect body roll. This spring was called a "camber compensator," which was standard on the S–90 and optional on all other models.

The Convertible D, built by Drauz, had become the Roadster in 1960, and was built through the 1961 and briefly into the 1962 model years. Early in 1961, Drauz was joined by d'Ieteren of Belgium in building Roadster bodies. At about the same time, Karmann began production of the hardtop Coupe (also called the notchback), which was similar in

The hardtop coupe built by Karmann in 1961 (T-5 body, shown) and 1962 (T-6 body) was based on the Cabriolet. The "B" pillar curves slightly to match the shape of the roll-up side window. This body style was never very popular when the cars were new so even though its production numbers were small, it isn't the collector item it theoretically should be. *Kurt Worner/Road & Track*

The 356B, in 1960 and '61, had the T-5 body with the high bumpers, raised-center hubcaps and headlights mounted higher on the front fenders which made the fender line straighter from the windshield to the top of the light (when compared to the 356A). The front compartment opening was rounded at the leading edge. Shown is a standard Cabriolet. *Porsche+Audi*

appearance to the removable hardtop Cabriolets; but this top was fixed permanently to the body shell, basically a Cabriolet. The Karmann Coupe body continued through 1962.

1962

Once again the new Porsche was updated without losing its character and traditional appearance, although the changes were significant from both an esthetic and practical point. When the 1962 356B (T–6 body) was shown at the Frankfurt show in September 1961, it displayed twin air-intake grilles in the rear lid, a larger windshield and rear window on the Coupe, an outside gas filler under a door in the right front fender, a new cowl vent, and a "flattened" lower edge of the front lid.

The battery moved to the right side of the front compartment and the optional gasoline heater nestled in the space formerly occupied by the battery. Fuel was put into the 13.2–gallon tank through a filler hidden under a door in the right front fender. This door was spring-loaded, and was opened from inside the car.

The fuel tank itself was no longer the familiar box that had been used since the first 356 coupe, but was now flatter and spread out over the floor of the front compartment. At the back of this compartment the fuse box was located, which had been inside the car, and a plastic container for windshield washer fluid.

A new fresh-air system was incorporated to allow better outside air intake to the occupants, by means of an intake air grille located in the center of the cowl. This put fresh air under the front hood where it was picked up by two air regulators—one on the right and one on the left of the hood hinges. The occupants could regulate the forced air either up through the defroster outlets or down under the dash. It was a far superior system to the one previously used and eliminated another customer complaint.

The Haussermann A–10 180 mm clutch was replaced by a larger A–12 200 mm model in the Super 90; and the 1600 Super engine had cast-iron instead of aluminum cylinders, as in the 1600.

Porsche transmissions were available with four different ratios for first, second and fourth gears, and five ratios for third. These were referred to as A, B, C, D and E gearing. Unless ordered otherwise, the 1962 Porsches came with a 7:31 axle (4.428:1 ratio) and BBBD transmission gearing. Also available for road cars were BBBC or BBAB gear sets. The seventeen transmission ratios and three axle ratios were mainly available to racers, who could change ratios to suit the course conditions, but there was really no reason for the average driver to need or want odd combinations of gearing; the factory did have it worked out pretty well for its road cars.

Also announced at the 1962 Porsche introduction, in September 1961, was the Carrera 2—still four cylinders with double overhead camshafts, but with a bore increase from 90 to 92 mm, and a stroke increase from 66 to 74 mm, resulting in a displacement of 1,966 cubic centimeters.

The two-liter Carrera retained the plain rod bearings of the previous Carrera, but the bearing diameter was reduced from 55 to 52 mm so the longer-stroke rods could clear the sides of the crankcase.

The fuel-level sending unit had been installed in the bottom of the new tank in the 1962 cars, but it all too often leaked, and was difficult to repair, so in February of 1962 the unit went back to the top of the tank.

1963

It had taken Porsche four years—from April 1950 until March 1954—to build and deliver the first 5,000 cars, but during the production years of the 356B, sales exceeded that figure each year: 1960—7,598; 1961—7,664; 1962—8,205; 1963—9,692 (includes 356C).

Running minor modifications continued to make Porsches gradually better each year for comfort, handling, driveability or ease of maintenance—sometimes in all areas.

Other changes were made, though, which would have a long-range effect on Porsche's design and production. In 1963, Porsche absorbed the Reutter body company, spinning off the seat-building division, which became Recaro (from *Reutter Carozzerie*, although it's not known why the original

German spelling, Karozzerie, was not used). In July, production started on the last 356 model, the C type.

In its April 15, 1960, road test of a 356B, *The Autocar* characterized Porsche: "When first presented to the public it was not an altogether good car on the road; it called for more than average skill—even courage—to get the best out of it. Over the years, various modifications to the suspension and steering gear have given the car progressively more orthodox handling characteristics."

Magazine road test reports were generally enthusiastic, sometimes to the degree that they sounded almost like press releases from the factory, but occasional criticism did crop up, as in this May 1960 report in *Sports Cars Illustrated*: "At the back, the exhaust pipes joggle through S-bends to get to the exits, which are integrated with—and which quickly discolor—the rear bumper guards."

The magazine's staff liked the interior, particularly the seating, but prefaced those comments with this: "There are many more detail changes inside the 356B. To discuss them we have to step inside, a process which, in itself, isn't easy."

Sports Cars Illustrated's European editor had purchased a new Super 90, and waxed eloquent about it: "But it's on the bumpy back roads that this car really performs wonders. You find yourself searching for serpentine, climbing, diving and winding byways just to exploit the astonishing agility of this car. The surface doesn't matter; the bumpier it is, the more the Porsche likes it."

In its May 3, 1962, issue *The Motor* testers said: "Thirteen years of development have left few if any of the original components unaltered but the general layout remains the same . . ." And, "The usual tendency for cars to grow in size and weight has been largely resisted and although increasing refinement has brought some weight penalty, the 17½-cwt [1,960-pound] car is one of the very few machines available to a buyer who insists on luxury in a compact and agile form."

Car and Driver's October 1963 report of a 356B listed a few criticisms, but on the whole, it was an extremely complimentary report, saying, among other things: "The

renovation brought about a car that has virtually neutral steering characteristics; handling so safe that only the most hapless, witless, inept driver could let the car get away from him (or, significantly, her—the Normal is called the 'ladies' model in German)." And, later: "A large measure of the car's excellent controllability is due to the command the driver has over his machine." The magazine's reference to the "ladies" model was about the "Damen," as the factory people called it.

356B (1960–63)

Engine

Design: . . . . Air-cooled flat (opposed) four
Type: 1600 . . . . . . 616/1, 3-piece crankcase, plain-bearing crank
  1600S . . . 1960–61: 616/2, 1962–63: 616/12, 3-piece crankcase, plain-bearing crank
  1600S-90 . . . . . 616/7, 3-piece crankcase, plain-bearing crank
Borexstroke, mm/inches: 1600, 1600S, 1600S-90 . . . . . . 82.5x74/ 3.25x2.91
Displacement, cc/cubic inches: 1600, 1600S, 1600S-90 . . . . 1582/96.5
Valve operation: . . . . . . Single camshaft with pushrods & rocker arms; inclined exhaust valves
Compression ratio: 1600 . . . . 7.5:1
  1600S 8.5:1
  1600S-90 . . . . 9:1
Carburetion: 1600, 1600S . . . . Two Zenith 32 NDIX
  1600S-90 . . . . Two Solex 40 PII-4
BHP (Mfr): 1600 . . . . 60 DIN/70 SAE @ 4500
  1600S . . . . 75 DIN/88 SAE @ 5000
  1600S-90 . . . . 90 DIN/102 SAE @ 5500

Chassis & drivetrain

Frame: . . . . . . Boxed-section pressed steel in unit with floor pan
Component layout: . . . . Rear engine, rear drive
Clutch: . . . . . . Haussermann single dry-plate (first cars), Fichtel & Sachs single dry-plate (from early 1960)
Transmission: . . . . Porsche four-speed, all-synchromesh (all gears indirect)
Axle ratio: 4.43:1
Rear suspension: . . . . . Independent (swing axle) with transverse torsion bars & telescopic shock absorbers
Front suspension: . . . . . Independent, with parallel trailing arms, transverse laminated torsion bars, telescopic shock absorbers & anti-roll bar

General

Wheelbase, mm/inches: 2100/82.7
Track, front, mm/inches: 1306/51.4
  rear, mm/inches: 1272/50.1
Brakes: . . . . Aluminum drums with iron liners
Tire size, front & rear: . . . . 1600S-90: 5.90-15, 1600 & 1600S: 5.60-15
Wheels: . . . . Bolt-on steel disc
Body builder: . . . . Coupe & Cabriolet: Reutter
  Roadster: 1960—Drauz, 1961–62—d'Ieteren
  Hardtop: 1961–62 Karmann
  Coupe: 1962–63—Karmann

Seen one, seen'em all? Not necessarily. Each year and model has subtleties; this 1962 356B Super 90 has a Fram oil filter, Knecht air filter and Bosch ignition—all standard Porsche equipment, but shapes and colors can make a difference. This engine also has an aftermarket fuel filter. *Mike Parris/Argus*

The 1962 T-6 body interior had the traditional Porsche look, with three instruments grouped in front of the driver, rubber floor mats and carpeted kick panels but now carried a VDO clock in the center of the panel and the heater/ventilation control above clock. *Mike Parris/Argus*

Finally, capping the report, the writer became positively eloquent: "A Porsche's excitement is as much intellectual as visceral; the pride and pleasure of ownership comes not only from its characteristic comfort, controllability and roadability, but also its freedom from temperament. Simply: the absence of pain. Its dependability can be taken as much for granted as that of a Chevy station wagon—you can toss in a girl and some luggage and shove off, never having any trepidation about the romance of the car, the road, the girl, being punctured by mechanical disaster. It's that kind of car."

Others might express it differently, but most owners felt that way about the 356B; and justifiably so. There are Porsche owners, even today, who don't see the need for disc brakes, and who consider the 356B as the best of the last "real Porsches."

The 356B received the T–6 body for 1962, as shown by the darker car at the right. It had a more squared-off front lid, twin rear-lid air intake grilles, and a larger rear window.

Chapter 5

356C

When production began on the 356C in July 1963, the car was visually little changed from the 356B of 1963. A close look, however, revealed a new wheel and hubcap design that covered four-wheel disc brakes—a Porsche first on a customer road car.

The Porsche company had been experimenting with disc brakes since 1958, testing two systems: Porsche's own design had the brake disc attached to the hub at its outer periphery (to utilize the open-center wheels carried over from Volkswagen) and the caliper was inside the disc. This assembly was light, weighing only a few ounces more per wheel than the older drum brake design. The Dunlop disc brakes, also being tested, were much heavier than either the Porsche disc or drum design; but when the decision was finally made to adopt disc brakes on the production cars, this was the system that won. The decision was primarily one based on cost and supply. Porsche would have been the only car company using its design, but most of the world's cars using disc brakes were utilizing the Dunlop design, made either by Dunlop or another company building them under license from Dunlop.

Porsche's disc brakes were supplied by Ate (Alfred Teves), manufactured under license from Dunlop. Some unique Porsche features were incorporated into the new brakes, the most significant being the mechanical parking brake working in a "hat section" which created a seven-inch-diameter drum inside the rear brake disc on each side.

Three engines were available in the C model: the Carrera 2, the 1600C and 1600SC—the latter two being derived from the 1600S and the Super 90, respectively.

Under Ing. Hans Mezger's direction, some significant engine changes were made. Intake valve diameter on the Super 90 was reduced from 40 to 38 mm, and exhaust valve diameter was increased from 31 to 34 mm.

The SC utilized the camshaft from the Super 90, and a new camshaft was developed for the 1600C which was similar to the 1600 cam, but with lift increased from 8.5 to 10 mm. The intake and exhaust ports on both engines were reshaped to give better flow.

At the start of 356C production, the 1600C engine had cast-iron cylinders, while the SC had Ferral-coated aluminum cylinders (also a holdover from the Super 90). But later in the 1964 model year, the SC was given yet a different cylinder treatment called Biral, which consisted of a cast-iron sleeve around which a finned aluminum "muff" was cast. This system, similar to the Alfin brake process, allowed much better heat dissipation from cylinder to air. It was better than cast-iron, and less expensive than the Ferral process.

The two engines had identical crankcases, with main bearing journals of 50–55–55–40 mm diameter, from flywheel to cranknose. The Super 90 crank was 55–55–55–40. The SC crankshaft had four integral counterweights which gave smoother running and, as a result, the maximum horsepower of 95 DIN was obtained at 5800 rpm.

The 356C is the best of the early Porsches, to drive or to look at; 15 years of development had made it into a great car. *Author*

At the same time, both engines were "Americanized" by adding tubing for positive crankcase ventilation; with the unburned hydrocarbons being sucked into the carburetor inlets of the right bank of cylinders.

After fifteen-and-a-half years and 76,303 Porsches of the Type 356, 356A, 356B and 356C, production stopped in September 1965. Factory records indicate that ten additional Cs were built for special customers in 1966. The C model was, in this writer's opinion, the best of the series, not only because continual development improved an already good car; but it was, and is, a better looking Porsche than were previous models.

Apparently magazine road testers agreed, because their comments and evaluations criticized less and less as time went on.

Car and Driver's staff presented a mixed review of the 356C in its 1965 *Car and Driver Yearbook*, on one hand accusing the company of needless cost cutting, while on the other heaping high praise on the Porsche engine

A 356C is distinguishable from the 356B by the flat hubcaps which go with the C's disc brakes.

These were not only the best of the 356 series, but the best looking. *Porsche Werkfoto*

and disc brakes. The testers lamented the loss of the camber compensator: "Again, Porsche says the cars don't 'need' it . . . and again, it's a patently transparent move to cut corners—in this instance, maybe $6 per car. Any individual buyer who feels he 'needs' a camber compensator may buy one as an after-market accessory . . . for about $65 plus installation (or less, with the car)." The C and SC could be special-ordered with the camber compensator for about $30 extra.

The writer qualified his remarks by saying: "We feel that Porsche enthusiasts have no use for second rate equipment—at any price. They strike us as being that rare kind of consumer who knows exactly what he wants, and who is willing to pay the going price to get it."

But about the engine and brakes, *Car and Driver's* minions had this to say: "With the 1964 models Porsche may have taken a step backwards in suspension equipment, but there has been a great leap forward in brakes, and the SC engine is unquestionably the best pushrod engine Porsche has ever built."

This would seem to be the consensus of most 356 enthusiasts, but there are those who disagree for some reason. Regardless of

356C (1964–65)

Engine
Design:	Air-cooled flat (opposed) four
Type: 1600C	616/15, 3-piece crankcase, plain-bearing crank
1600SC	616/16, 3-piece crankcase, plain-bearing crank
Borexstroke, mm/inches: 1600C, 1600SC	82.5x74/3.25x2.91
Displacement, cc/cubic inches: 1600C, 1600SC	1582/96.5
Valve operation:	Single camshaft with pushrods & rocker arms; inclined exhaust valves
Compression ratio: 1600C	8.5:1
1600SC	9.5:1
Carburetion: 1600C	Two Zenith 32 NDIX
1600SC	Two Solex 40 PII-4
BHP (Mfr): 1600	75 DIN/88 SAE @ 5200
1600SC	95 DIN/107 SAE @ 5800

Chassis & drivetrain
Frame:	Boxed-section pressed steel in unit with floor pan
Component layout:	Rear engine, rear drive
Clutch:	Fichtel & Sachs single dry-plate
Transmission:	Porsche four-speed, all-synchromesh (all gears indirect)
Axle ratio:	4.43:1
Rear suspension:	Independent (swing axle) with transverse torsion bars & telescopic shock absorbers
Front suspension:	Independent, with parallel trailing arms, transverse laminated torsion bars, telescopic shock absorbers & anti-roll bar

General
Wheelbase, mm/inches:	2100/82.7
Track, front, mm/inches:	1306/51.4
rear, mm/inches:	1272/50.1
Brakes:	Ate disc
Tire size, front & rear:	5.60-15
Wheels:	Bolt-on steel disc
Body builder:	Cabriolet: Reutter, Coupe: Reutter & Karmann

A flat hubcap, this one with an enameled Porsche crest (some had metal crests, and some had no embellishment on the cap—see preceding page), identified a disc-braked 356C. *Author*

This dash shot of an early 1964 356C shows the glovebox, grab handle and padded sun visors available on the C series. On later 1964 models the handgrip was eliminated and the light switch moved from behind the steering wheel where it was easier to reach. *Porsche Werkfoto*

personal preference, the 356C was and is the most highly developed of the line, and with that development came a combination of more comfort and better and more effortless performance. The C model is better looking, and more mechanically "civilized" than any of its predecessors. It is the car I would like to own of this series, because with it you get more of the better Porsche qualities, and fewer of the poorer qualities.

Porsche's own disc brake design, sometimes referred to as a "ring disc" brake, had the caliper on the inside, with the disc and hub attached at their peripheries in order to utilize the wide bolt pattern of the early Porsche wheels. In spite of this brake's light weight, limited production would have made the unit cost extremely high. It was used on the F-1 cars and the Carrera 2. *Author*

Disc brake and caliper for the 356C were made by Ate under license from Dunlop. The rear disc incorporated a small drum-type parking brake which was operated mechanically. *Author*

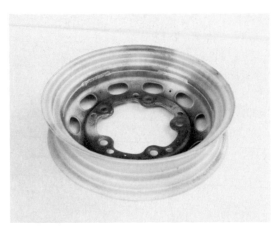

The 3¼-inch-wide wheels of the 356 had the rim and wheel center welded together and carried the large-diameter bolt circle to match the Volkswagen brake drums used on the early cars. *Author*

Alloy rim wheels, either 4½- or five-inch-wide rims, were riveted together; and even though Porsche now had its own wheels, the bolt pattern was the same as the older wheels made to fit VW drums. *Author*

The 4½J-15 wheel for the 356C was all steel and welded together as with other Porsche steel wheels. The bolt circle was smaller than before due to the hubs used with the new disc brakes on the C models. *Author*

Carrera wheel, left, has steel center and 4½-inch-15 alloy rim, while the 356A is a 4½-15 all-steel wheel. The Carrera wheel has different offset to allow for 20-mm-wider drum. *Author*

Squeaky-clean 356C being shown at a concours with all the original tools, spares and owners manual—all rare items on a 17-year-old car. *Author*

No doubt about the year or type. *Author*

★★★★★

Chapter 6

356 Carrera

The first Porsche Carrera was introduced along with the 356A at the Frankfurt auto show in September 1955; but the concept of the car goes back to 1952. Ferry Porsche and his team of engineers had wondered what the potential of the air-cooled four-cylinder boxer engine might be, and Dr. Ernst (later to be Prof.) Fuhrmann was told to find out. A figure of 70 hp per liter had been spoken of, and Fuhrmann's calculations indicated the figure was possible—with four camshafts instead of the single camshaft and push-rod/rocker-arm valve actuation.

The Fuhrmann design followed the basic configuration of the standard Porsche engine, but differed in almost every detail. It had four camshafts (two per side, called double overhead, or dohc), twin ignition, dual twin-choke Solex carburetors, dry-sump lubrication, and roller bearings on both mains and rods.

The use of roller bearings in a racing engine has been debated by engineers for many years and there is still no clear-cut answer to the question about advantages versus disadvantages. Dr. Porsche had used roller bearings for the connecting rod big-ends of the Auto Union (the upper end of the rods rode on needle bearings around the wrist pins), so there was precedent even within the Porsche organization. Fuhrmann used rollers to get a stronger single-piece connecting rod, and because there was no need for high oil pressure at high rpm in the four-cam engine. When roller bearings were

introduced in the pushrod engine (see Chapter One), it was done to achieve a longer stroke within an existing crankcase.

Fuhrmann's new design was tested on Maundy Thursday, 1953. It was a happy day for several reasons: It was three years to the day after the first Stuttgart-built Porsche 356 (1100 cc and 38 hp) rolled out of the Porsche works, and the new engine produced 112 hp at 6400 rpm on the first test of this 1498 cc engine; 74 hp per liter.

"These first four-cam engines took a skilled man 120 hours to assemble a complete engine, and the timing alone could take eight hours—sometimes fifteen," Fuhrmann recalled, "if tolerances weren't just right." The first few race engine builders trained another twenty to twenty-five mechanics from among Porsche's best to assemble four-cam engines when the Carrera came along.

The first competition appearance of the engine was at the Nürburgring in August 1953, where the car practiced but didn't race. A week later, the same car ran at the Freiburg hill climb and finished third, driven by Auto Union ace Hans Stuck. The engine was originally planned for the 550 Spyder (1500A/550RS); but in March 1954, one of the four-cam Type 547 engines was installed in Prof. Porsche's personal car, *Ferdinand*, to evaluate the engine/chassis combination.

In August 1954, a Le Mans-type four-cam was put in a Gmünd-built coupe for the Liege-Rome-Liege rally and, driven by Helmut Polensky and Herbert Linge, won out-

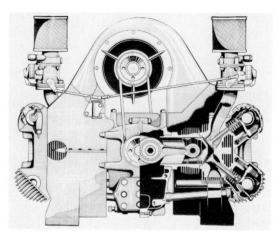

Basic layout of the 550 Spyder engine, forerunner of the Carrera engine, including the cams, valves and springs, pistons, roller-bearing rods and crankshaft. Not shown here are the nine shafts, 14 bevel gears and two spur wheels it took to drive the valve train. *Porsche Werkfoto*

right victory. Porsche was still experimenting with this powerful engine and in the summer of 1955 installed a 547 engine in Ferdinand Porsche's gray Cabriolet. The enthusiasm was universal from Porsche personnel, only Fuhrmann having had expectations of this possibility right from the start.

When the Carrera made its debut at Frankfurt in 1955, as the 1500GS, it had the 547/1 engine which was almost identical to the 1500RS Spyder power plant, with two Solex 40 PII carburetors, 8.7:1 compression ratio (it was raised to 9:1 by 1957) and produced 100 DIN horsepower.

The engine, unlike the pushrod 356, was dry-sumped, with the oil tank in the left rear fender. An 8000-rpm tach and a 250-km/h speedometer were fitted. Also included in the instrument panel were two switches which controlled the current to the dual

The 1956 Carrera owned by John von Neumann was painted silver with a red stripe down the front hood and body. John's company, Competition Motors, was the Porsche/VW distributor for the Southwest, and John was a regular and successful racer in West Coast sports car events driving MG, Porsche and Ferrari at various times. *Ralph Poole*

59

coils. These switches were used mainly to check the ignition system as the engine normally ran on both coils and the two spark plugs per cylinder. The distributors were driven from the ends of the camshafts.

The four-cam engine was available in all three body styles, and the cars weighed a bit over 100 pounds more than the comparable car with a pushrod four. Weight distribution was forty-one percent front, fifty-nine percent rear.

Carrera owners were advised to keep the revs above 2500 and below 6500 for normal, or sustained, driving; but the engine would run to 7500 and would accept full throttle at 1500 rpm.

The Carrera was distinguished from the normal Porsches by the gold Carrera script on the rear deck (and front fenders of the 356A), and the dual exhausts under the rear bumper. A close look would also reveal the screen in front of the dry-sump tank behind the left rear wheel.

In 1956 it was felt that the Carrera was neither luxurious enough for a comfortable road car nor light enough for a racer. In May 1957, the Carrera line was divided into Deluxe and GT (the latter available only as a stripped Coupe, or Speedster, with bucket seats, plastic windows, lighter bumpers, Nardi wood-rimmed aluminum steering wheels and Spyder front brakes which had 60-mm-wide drums instead of the normal 40 mm drums). No creature comforts were included in the GT, not even a heater. A GT Speedster was offered with Weber carburetors, twenty-one-gallon fuel tank, and an engine producing 110 DIN horsepower at 6400 rpm. Three axle ratios, 4.428, 4.85 or 5.167:1, were available.

1958

In September 1957, the T-2 body became the standard Porsche configuration for all models, pushrod or four-cam, but the Carrera didn't have the exhaust through the rear bumper guards as did the pushrod cars. The removable hardtop version was available in Carrera Deluxe form and was continued until the phase-out of the 356A in 1959.

The 1958 Carrera GT had aluminum doors, and front and rear lids. The engine was now the Type 692/2, with plain bearings and two distributors driven from the front of the crank (actually, the rear of the car). A larger bore, of 87.5 mm, and a 66 mm stroke gave a displacement of 1587 cc. The engine in the Deluxe model had a compression ratio of 9.5:1 while the GT version had 9.8:1. The GT engine also had sodium-filled exhaust valves. Because of the plain bearings, oil pressure had to be raised over that of the roller-bearing engines and this was accomplished by widening the gears in the oil pump. To combat higher oil temperatures, two oil coolers, mounted in front behind the horn grilles, were incorporated into the dry-sump system.

The early 1958 Carrera engines were the Type 692/0 roller-bearing units which had 1500 cc and 110 hp at 6400 rpm. Twenty of these engines were made. Then came the 692/1 which also had 1500 cc, but plain bearings. It also developed 110 hp at 6400, and fourteen of these were built. The 692/2 was a 1600 cc engine which had "only" 105 hp at 6500.

1959

The most luxurious Porsche to date, the 356A/1600GS Carrera, was brought out in 1959. It had the 692/2 engine and, with its deluxe trim, weighed 2,100 pounds. Production of the 356A Carrera Type 692/2 engines amounted to forty-five in 1958, forty-seven in 1959 and only two in 1960.

1960

Porsche wanted to remain competitive and the Carreras were getting heavier while the competition was getting lighter. In 1960, Porsche entered into an agreement with Zagato (with Carlo Abarth as intermediary) to build some lightweight Carreras. These cars, called the Abarth Carrera GTL, were the fastest GT Porsches yet, and were successful in both racing and rallying. Meanwhile, Porsche had asked Reutter for a bid on forty bodies of either the T-2 or T-5 configuration (depending on which the Federation Internationale de l'Automobile would approve for competition). As a result, a series of T-5 bodies was built for the Carrera.

For the 1960 and 1961 model years, only lightweight GT Carrera Coupes were made with the Reutter bodywork. Outwardly

This von Neumann 1956 Carrera interior has a 160 mph speedometer, 8000 rpm tach, oil temperature and fuel gauges. Light-beam-change button is next to clutch pedal and the windshield washer pump actuator is above that on the toeboard. Upholstery is leather with carpeted kick panels and rubber floor mats. *Ralph Poole*

Oil cooler mounted in the rear fender of this 1956 Carrera has screen to let in air but keep out the larger pieces of gravel. *Ralph Poole*

You had *arrived* when your Porsche carried this gold script on the fender flank.

these Reutter-bodied Carreras could be mistaken for production Porsches, but they had simpler, lighter bumpers without vertical guards, aluminum hubcaps, bucket seats, less interior trim, and aluminum doors and hood/deck lids.

These cars had the Type 692/3 engine in 1960, and the 692/3A engine in 1961. The 692/3 series had Weber 40 DCM2 carburetors, and a 12-volt electrical system—the first Carrera so equipped. The 692/3 engine produced 115 DIN/145 SAE horsepower at 6500 rpm. A total of 700 Carreras had been built up to January 1960.

With the advent of the 692/3A engine in 1961, the main bearing journals were enlarged from 55 to 60 mm in diameter, and the rod journals were left at 55 mm, but stronger rods were used.

When the 692 engine was first introduced, with its crank-driven distributors, a torsional vibration set in at about 7000 rpm and this was cured by the addition of six small flywheels on the 692/3A engine. Four of these flywheels, each about 45 mm in diameter, were attached to the exhaust camshafts, and two, of about 75 mm diameter, were attached to the inlet camshafts. The purpose was to dampen the harmonic vibration out of the valve train.

At the Frankfurt show in September 1961, the last 356 Carrera made its debut. This was the fastest Porsche 356 road car built, although the factory still claimed only a 125-mile-per-hour top speed—the Carrera 2000 GS. It went on sale in April 1962 as the Carrera 2.

The engine had 1966 cc and produced 130 bhp at 6200 rpm. It was not only the fastest road Porsche to date, but it was also the most demanding of the driver because of its extra power and the extremely tail-heavy weight distribution. It took an expert driver to realize the maximum potential from the Carrera 2.

A bit of aid in this area was provided by the addition of Porsche's first disc brakes on a road car. These were of Porsche design, and carried the cast-iron caliper (alloy on the racing cars) inside the ring disc, which carried the wheel bolted to its outer circumference to utilize the wide-spaced wheel attachments

common to Porsches then. This was a carryover from Volkswagen and allowed a much lighter wheel (contributing to low unsprung weight), but heat transfer from the brake disc to the wheel after prolonged hard use—such as racing—caused fatigue cracks around the disc attachment holes.

The Carrera 2 won races, and rallies, but was short-lived; the main reason for its existence seemed to be to legitimize a two-liter engine in the Abarth Carrera, which had started out as a 1600. So few Abarths were made, about twenty, that they were reengined as the factory or private owners deemed necessary to meet competition.

But by this time, racing had gotten so specialized that a dual-purpose car of this type was not a guaranteed race winner any longer. The Carrera in normal 356 body form gave way to specialized factory racers; first the 2000 GS/GT and then the 904 GTS.

Aside from driving skills necessary to achieve utmost performance from a four-cam Carrera, service and maintenance also became a problem. The first time the Porsche service chief looked into the engine compartment at the four-cam engine, he supposedly slammed the cover down with the comment "How can I change spark plugs I can't even find?" And there were eight to change! In Jerry Sloniger's fine book *Porsche: The 4-Cylinder, 4-Cam Sports & Racing Cars*, he says there was talk among Porsche people of hiring an asbestos octopus to change the plugs.

In its September 1956 road test report on a 356A 1500 GS, *Road & Track*'s writer said: "In addition, the Carreras appear to be coming through with a torsion bar setting which gives about one degree of negative camber at the rear wheels, with no load. This, and the larger 5.90" section road racing tires give as close to neutral steering as is conceivable." But then: "High speed stability at over 100 mph in a cross wind still leaves something to be desired, in our opinion, but this applies to almost any well-streamlined coupe with preponderance of weight on the rear wheels."

The Autocar, in a "used car" road test in June 1964, had this to say about the former Dick Stoop 1600 Carrera (a 1960 model): "It goes without saying for a Porsche that, although this car had travelled far and fast (the speedometer recorded just under 37,000 miles), there was not a creak, rattle or any sign of movement in the body structure." A great recommendation for a road/race car—or any sporting car for that matter.

Top Gear magazine (England) reported on the Carrera Speedster in a 1958 issue: "On the autobahnen, which are not always smoothly surfaced, we discovered that bumps which would rock a more normally suspended sports car on its rebound stops became smoother as speed was increased. It was in fact possible to cruise this 1½ litre motor car at a true 100 m.p.h. for long distances on the autobahn, and, the greater the speed, the smoother the ride."

John Bentley, writing in *Foreign Cars Illustrated*, October 1958, said: "I became convinced of one thing: any competition driver searching for the true all-purpose sports car—one that you could drive to the A & P and then race over the weekend—need not bother to look any further than the Carrera."

Bentley liked the Carrera so much that he bought a 1958 Carrera Speedster, but then trouble, rather than fun, began. After breaking-in the car according to the manual (no more than 4500 rpm for the first 750 miles and not over 5000 rpm for the next 2,400 miles) ". . . the car seemed to lose all its pep and would not pull the skin off a rice pudding in any gear." The rings had not seated properly in Bentley's engine, and it was subsequently pulled down and rebuilt under warranty. "Now," said the factory representative, "go out and beat the hell out of it. Take it to 7000 rpm if you like—just for short bursts. But don't baby the engine. This is a Carrera GT!"

What Bentley hadn't known before, but found out then, was that Carrera engines were bench-tested at 4000 rpm for several hours and given a full-throttle test that lasted several minutes, before the engine was installed in a car.

Writing in the September 1959 issue of *Sports Cars Illustrated* Jesse Alexander wrote of the 1600 Carrera GS: "By the end of our trip [more than 1,000 miles], we had added exactly three quarts of oil, apparently a good figure judging from the experience of other Carrera owners with whom we talked." But Jesse liked the Carrera, and finished his report by saying: "As in any car, the Carrera had its failings—most troublesome was its inability to get off the mark smartly without slipping the clutch. Apart from this, we enjoyed driving the car tremendously; she'll cruise all day long at 100 mph and is equally at home in the midst of city traffic. With the

Rear of the 1958 Carrera looked almost like the pushrod Porsches of the same period, but dual exhaust tips were under the bumper instead of through the lower end of the uprights. *Porsche Werkfoto*

Left, 40-mm-wide 356A brake shoe and drum, compared to the 60-mm-wide Carrera shoe and drum. *Author*

It was often easier to remove the Carrera engine than it was to work on it in the car. This was a private entry at the Eberbach hillclimb in 1962. *Kurt Worner/Road & Track*

A Carrera 356A Coupe, which the high front bumper "bow" identifies as a late 1959 unless the owner has added it later. The rear view mirrors are after-market items. The deluxe hubcaps were standard on the Carrera GS, but were often added to other models by owners.

The Carrera 2 carried the same body configuration as other "B" series 356s, with the high front fenders and headlights, squared-off front and rear lids, wider front hood handle, twin air intake grilles at the back, and raised bumpers. In addition, the Carrera had the twin pipes poking through an apron below the rear body. *Argus*

Carrera's flexibility in the gears, one is able to overtake or to shoot through narrow gaps almost at will—all in all a very satisfying car to drive."

The 356 Carrera variants were fantastic cars for their time—or any other time, probably. They were fast, comfortable and reliable. Both owners and magazine road testers were impressed by the Carrera's mechanical state-of-the-art design, and spectators at road races had to be impressed with its racing performance. And as a collector car, the Carrera has to be one of the most desirable, if costly, vehicles.

356-based Carrera

Engine
Design: .... Air-cooled flat (opposed) four
Borexstroke, mm/inches: 356, 356A, 1500GS, GS GT
& GS Deluxe 85x66/3.35x2.60
1600 GS GT, Abarth GTL I & II 87.5x66/3.45x2.60
Carrera 2B, 2C, C-GT, 2000 GS-GT & 904 GTS ....
92x74/3.62x2.92
Displacement, cc/cubic inches: 356, 356A, 1500GS,
& GS Deluxe 1498/91.4
1600GS GT, Abarth GTL I & II 1587/96.8
Carrera 2B, 2C, C-GT, 2000 GS-GT & 904 GTS ... 1966/119.9
Valve operation: .... Gear & shaft-driven twin camshafts
on each bank; inclined valves
Compression ratio: 356, 356A, 1500GS, GS-GT 9.0:1
GS Deluxe, Carrera 2B & 2C, C-GT 9.5:1
1600GS GT Abarth GTL I & II, 2000 GS-GT, 904 GTS ... 9.8:1
Carburetion: 356, 365A, 1500GS, GS-GT ..... Two Solex 40 PJJ
356A GS Deluxe .... Two Solex 40 PJJ-4
1600S GT, Abarth GTL I ...... Two Weber 40 DCM 2
Carrera 2B & 2C, Abarth GTL II .... Two Solex 40 P-II-4
C-GT, 2000 GS-GT, 904 GTS .... Two Weber 46 IDM 2
BHP (Mfr): 356, 356A 1500 GS .... 100 DIN/115 SAE @ 6200
356A GS-GT .... 110 DIN/127 SAE @ 6400
356A GS Deluxe .... 105 DIN/121 SAE @ 6500
1600 GS-GT .... 115 DIN/132 SAE @ 6500
Carrera 2B & 2C .... 130 DIN/150 SAE @ 6200
356C-GT .... 160 DIN/184 SAE @ 6500
Abarth GTL .... 115 DIN/132 SAE @ 6500
Abarth GTL I .... 128 DIN/147 SAE @ 6700
Abarth GTL II .... 135 DIN/155 SAE @ 7400
2000 GS GT .... 155 DIN/178 SAE @ 7800
904 GTS (road) .... 155 DIN/178 SAE @ 6400
904 GTS (race) .... 180 DIN/207 SAE @ 7000
Chassis & drivetrain
Frame: 904 .... Boxed-section ladder-type frame (bonded to
fiberglass body)
All others .... Boxed-section pressed steel in unit with
floor pan
Component layout: 904 .... Mid engine, rear drive

All others .... Rear engine, rear drive
Clutch: 356, 356A 1500GS ..... Fichtel & Sachs K12 200 single
dry-plate
356A GS GT, GS Deluxe, 1600 GS GT, Carrera 2B ....
Haussermann A-10 single dry-plate
All others .... Haussermann A-12 single dry-plate
Transmission: 904 GTS ... Porsche five-speed, all- synchromesh
All others .... Porsche four-speed, all synchromesh
Axle ratio: 4.428:1
Rear suspension: 904 ..... Independent, with reversed A-arms,
trailing links, coil springs, tubular shock absorbers
& anti-roll bar
All others .... Independent (swing axle) with transverse
torsion bars & telescopic shock absorbers
Front suspension: 904 ...... Independent, with upper and lower
A-arms, coil springs, tubular shock absorbers & anti-roll bar
All others .... Independent, with parallel trailing arms,
transverse laminated torsion bars, shock absorbers &
(after 1954) anti-roll bar
General
Wheelbase, mm/inches (356-based): 2100/82.7
904 .... 2300/90.6
Track, front, mm/inches: 356 .... 1290/50.8
904 GTS 1314/51.7
All others 1306/51.4
rear, mm/inches: 356 .... 1250/49.2
904 GTS 1312/51.6
All others 1272/50.1
Brakes: .... 356, 356A 1500GS, GS-GT, 1600 GS-GT, drum
(Carrera 2s had Porsche ring discs)
Carrera 2C, C-GT, Abarth GTL, GTL I & II, 2000 GS-GT ......
Porsche ring-disc
904 GTS .... Dunlop/Ate disc
Tire size, front & rear: 356 .... 5.00–16
356A 1500GS, GS-GT, GS Deluxe 5.90–16
1600GS-GT, Abarth GTL, GTL I & II, 2000 GS-GT 5.90–15
Carrera 2B, 2C & C-GT 165–15
904 GTS 5.50/6.00–15
Wheels: .... Stamped steel disc
Body builder: Abarth GTL, GTL I & II .... Abarth
904 GTS .... Heinkel
All others .... Reutter

Carrera engines didn't leave much room for mechanics to work—prompting the factory joke of hiring an asbestos octopus to change spark plugs. A 1600 Carrera engine, from the front, complete with flywheel, pressure plate and clutch disc. The double-entry fan can just be seen. *Porsche Werkfoto*

Carrera 2 Cabriolet and Coupe are rare and valuable cars, even more so today than when new. These are cars to be shown, treasured and kept at home the rest of the time out of harm's way, unless you're the type who can stand the emotional trauma of a possible side-swipe or caved-in rear end from an inattentive driver.

★★	1965–74
★★★	1975–on
★★★★	Carrera

901/911

It was evident to Porsche management as early as the mid-fifties that the 356 series would someday come to an end. The body shape was becoming dated, and the four-cylinder pushrod engine was reaching the end of its potential. The four-cam Carrera engine was considered briefly as an across-the-board replacement for the pushrod and rocker arm engine, but was too costly and too complicated to be considered seriously for general use.

In 1959, Ferdinand "Butzi" Porsche (Ferry's son) started designing a body for the new car. His father had decreed that the new Porsche would be an evolutionary design, to continue in the established Porsche tradition, would have no more than a 2,200 mm wheelbase (100 mm longer than the 356), and would carry two adult passengers and two children in small rear seats with folding seatbacks to accommodate more luggage if only two persons were aboard.

Reutter and old Porsche stalwart Erwin Komenda shared the responsibility of preparing the car for production.

The new car was introduced at the Frankfurt auto show in September 1963 as the Porsche 901. The 901 met all the criteria set by Dr. Porsche: It had a family resemblance to previous models, it was more powerful, smoother, more comfortable, quieter, had more space for people and luggage and was only minimally larger than the 356. The wheelbase had grown from 2,100 to 2,211 mm (from 82.7 to 87.04 inches), and overall

length had increased 153 mm (from 158 to 163.8 inches), but width had decreased by 60 mm (from 65.8 to 63.4 inches).

The body structure was similar to that of the 356, utilizing an all-steel form welded into a single unit-body chassis. Front suspension had a MacPherson strut and lower wishbone with a longitudinal torsion bar on each side, and an anti-roll bar connecting the two sides. Torsion bars were also used at the rear, but mounted transversely, and the suspension members were triangulated trailing links. The rear axles, unlike the 356, had inner and outer U-joints. Tubular shock absorbers were used all around, and the brakes were almost identical to the last 356's: Ate-built discs with the parking brakes working inside drums in the rear brake discs.

The steering was ZF rack and pinion, with two universal joints in the column, which connected to the steering rack at its center. Two purposes were served by the design: It made left- or right-hand-drive models easier to assemble, and the double-jointed column was a safety feature in a front end accident.

In debating the power plant, and its subsequent location in the new car, Dr. Porsche felt that front-engined cars were likely to become less popular, and a mid-engined design was impractical for general customer road use. Therefore, the engine, if light enough, should remain at the rear. Remember, he was thinking of high performance sports and GT cars, not four-door sedans, and the 356 replacement was destined to be a sports car in the established Porsche tradition.

The new engine, designed by Dr. Porsche's nephew, Ferdinand Piech, and developed by Hans Tomala, was an opposed six-cylinder unit with single chain-driven overhead camshafts—one on each bank—and two inclined valves per cylinder. Intake was through two triple-choke Solex floatless carburetors, and the car had a 12-volt electrical system.

Cast aluminum was used for the crankcase, a forged steel crankshaft ran in eight bearings (with a bearing between each cylinder) and the oiling system was of the dry-sump type. This was not only an aid to engine cooling, but resulted in a bit more ground clearance because a shallower sump could be used.

The 1991 cc engine produced 130 DIN and 148 SAE horsepower at 6100 rpm, and drove through a Fichtel & Sachs single dry-plate clutch to an all-synchromesh, five-speed transmission. The shift pattern was confusing to old Porsche hands, because second, third, fourth and fifth were in the normal H pattern, while first was down and to the left, with reverse high to the left above first. The shift was not difficult, once accustomed to it, but if the driver often drove other manual-shift cars with the old-style pattern, or was in a hurry, he very often tried to start out in second, thinking he was in first.

The 901 rode on fifteen-inch steel disc wheels with 4.5-inch-wide rims carrying 15-165 radial tires. Weight was up to 2,380 pounds, 405 of which were engine, clutch and engine accessories.

Before the new Porsche went into production in the fall of 1964, the name had been changed to 911, because Peugeot had copyrighted all combinations of three numbers with a zero in the middle. Peugeot was not only an old, respected company, but France was an excellent market for Porsche, so Porsche acquiesced to Peugeot's demands. Strangely enough, Peugeot had not objected to the Porsche 904—possibly because it was a racing model and not intended for production other than enough to meet the FIA minimum requirements (100 cars)—so Porsche hastily numbered subsequent competition cars 906 and 908.

One body style was all one could get on the early 911 but in September 1965, the Targa was introduced at the Frankfurt show. At this time, Wilhelm Karmann GmbH joined the Reutter division of Porsche as a producer of Porsche bodies. The demand for 911s had been such that Porsche's capacity was inadequate to keep up with sales. The first right-hand-drive 911, for the U.K. market, was made.

In July 1965, transmission gears were changed to a higher ratio (lower gear) and

The early 911 models, like this 1968, were devoid of the garnishment that was to give later models more pizzazz—fender flares, alloy wheels, spoilers, whale-tails and so on—but were also some of the cleanest looking of the series. *Porsche+Audi*

maximum speed was attained at 6700 instead of 6500 rpm. This gearing was the same as the 912 and the four-speed transmission was the standard production unit.

Early 911 customers had complained about front-end float and handling, because even with an extremely tail-heavy weight bias, the combined suspension design and narrow wheels and tires caused understeer unless the car was really pushed, at which time violent oversteer was induced without warning. The factory cure for this, for customers who could bring the car back to the factory, was to install an eleven-kilogram (24.2 pounds) cast-iron weight at each end of the front bumper. These weights were bolted and glued (to prevent vibration) inside the front bumper contour and flush with the backside so that the majority of owners never knew what had been done to cure the front end "float."

Owners also complained of fouled plugs after driving in traffic, and severe carburetion "flat spots" from the floatless Solex carburetors. In February 1966, Weber 40 IDA 3C carburetors replaced the Solexes. This eliminated the necessity for two mechanical fuel pumps, in addition to a Bendix electric pump, because the Webers had float bowls, and one Bendix pump was subsequently used. The Webers also had flat spots, and this problem was cured by the addition of adjustable accelerator pump rods.

1967

When the 1967 models went into production in July 1966, a new 911, the "S" model, was introduced. With new camshafts, larger valves, better porting, 9.8:1 compression ratio and Weber 40 IDS carburetors, the 911S produced 160 DIN and 180 SAE horsepower at 6600 rpm. An anti-roll bar was added at the rear, Koni shocks were standard as were vented brake discs, and the five-spoke Fuchs alloy wheels (which were five-pounds-per-wheel lighter than the steel wheels) made their Porsche debut.

Porsche management had thought that some sort of automatic transmission—one that would allow clutchless shifting without losing the Porsche sporting feel—should be developed for the American market. In 1967, the Sportomatic was introduced. This trans-

mission, the Type 905, developed by Fichtel & Sachs, had a three-element hydraulic torque converter and a four-speed transmission connected by a single dry-plate clutch.

Performance was altered only minimally, and it was felt that the American driver would take to this clutchless shifting (a switch in the gearshift knob was connected by a solenoid to a vacuum reservoir and the clutch was disengaged by merely touching the shift lever). In 1975, the Sportomatic became a three-speed unit when the three-liter engine was introduced, but the system was phased out in May 1979, rejected by the American buyers—the very market it was designed to conquer.

In typical Porsche fashion, odd models popped up from time to time that *may* have been intended for production and were most certainly planned for competition. One of these was the 911R, in 1967. The R had plastic front fenders, doors, hood and deck lids, and bumpers; plexiglass windows; and the sheet metal that was left was thinner than normal. The R's weight was under 2,000 pounds. Aided by 10.3:1 compression ratio and 46 mm Webers, the horsepower was 210 at 8000 rpm. It is my understanding that only twenty R models were built.

1968

In August 1967, when the A series 911s were introduced as the 1968 models, a lower-priced 911T came into the program for the European market. It had cast-iron cylinders instead of aluminum and a crankshaft with no counterweights. Steel rocker arms were replaced by cast-iron rockers, compression ratio was lowered to 8.6:1, and a milder camshaft was used. This 110–horsepower 911 had solid steel disc brake rotors instead of the vented type, steel wheels, four-speed transmission and a lighter front anti-roll bar. The interior was similar to the 912.

The 911S was available only in Europe in 1968 as it failed to meet the U.S. emission standards, and the other U.S. emission-equipped models were not up to Porsche's running standards; the air injection pump caused the engine to backfire. Porsche later produced a kit to correct these faults and it is unlikely that many 1968 911s have escaped the conversion. If you find one that hasn't been corrected, it can still be done.

The poor running of these cars was due mainly to inadequate carburetor jetting. This is where the adjustable accelerator rods came into play. Many manufacturers were in the same performance predicament. U.S. specs were slow in coming and reduction of jetting, even to the point of poor performance, seemed the only solution. Only 911s and 911Ls were brought to the United States in 1962. Mechanically the same, the L had the more luxurious S trim.

1969–1971

When production started on the 1969 B-series 911 in August 1968, the wheelbase had been stretched 57 mm (2.24 inches), to 2,268 mm. The increase was obtained by lengthening the rear trailing arms, but the engine and transmission remained in their original positions in the chassis. The old Nadella axle shafts were replaced by Löbro shafts with Rzeppa constant-velocity joints, and the shafts were canted rearward from the inner to outer joints. The result was a better weight distribution—from 41.5 front/58.5 rear to 43/57—and a much better ride, although part of the better weight distribution had to be from the use of two batteries in the front of the car.

B models included the 911, 911T (which was new to the U.S. market), 911E (which

By 1969, when the 57-mm-longer-wheelbase 911 B series came out, all models had fender flares as shown on this 1969 911T. *Porsche+Audi*

The 1969 911S, with its Fuchs five-spoke, forged-alloy wheels that were introduced on the model in 1967. The S model and the alloy wheels were two of Porsche's most popular products. *Porsche+Audi*

replaced the L) and the 911S. Brake discs on the E and S were ventilated, and were thicker, which widened the track about 0.4 inch. To accommodate the wider track, the wheel openings were flared, and this styling was carried on all 1969 versions of the 911. The S now had six-inch rims as standard equipment, and the E was equipped with Boge hydro-pneumatic, self-leveling front struts which eliminated the torsion bars (although many have since been converted to torsion bar suspension).

911, 911L, 911T, 911E, 911S (1965–68)
Engine
Design: .... Air-cooled flat (opposed) six
Borexstroke, mm/inches: 80x66/3.15x2.60
Displacement, cc/cubic inches: 1991/121.5
Valve operation: ...... Chain-driven single overhead camshaft
   on each bank with rocker arms & inclined valves
Compression ratio: 911, 911L 9:1
  911T 8.6:1
  911S 9.8:1
  911E 9.1:1
  911S (1968 Europe) 9.9:1
Carburetion: 911 .... Six Solex 40 PI
  911T, 911L, 911E .... Two Weber 40 IDA
  911S .... Two Weber 40 IDS
BHP (Mfr): 911, 911L, 911E .... 130 DIN/148 SAE @ 6100
  911S .... 160 DIN/180 SAE @ 6600
  911T .... 110 DIN/125 SAE @ 5800

Chassis & drivetrain
Frame: .... Unit body
Component layout: .... Rear engine, rear drive
Clutch: .... Fichtel & Sachs single dry-plate
Transmission: 1965 .... Porsche five-speed
  1966 .... Porsche four-speed (five-speed optional)
  1967-68 ..... Porsche four- or five-speed (optional F&S four-
   speed Sportomatic)
Axle ratio: 911T, 911E (with Sportomatic) 3.86:1
  911T, 911E (with standard four-speed or 911S five-speed)
  .... 4.43:1
  911T, 911E, 911S (optional with four- or five-speed trans)
  .... 4.833 or 4.38:1
Rear suspension: 911, 911T .... Independent, semi-trailing link
  on each side with transverse torsion bars & telescopic
  shock absorbers (911S, add anti-roll bar)
Front suspension: 911T MacPherson telescopic shock strut
  and triangulated wishbone on each side with longitudinal torsion
  bars (911 & 911S add anti-roll bar)

General
Wheelbase, mm/inches: 2211/87.1
Track, front, mm/inches: 1367/53.8
  rear, mm/inches: 911L, 911S 1339/52.7 (911T 1335/52.5)
Brakes: ... 911T Ate solid disc (911, 911L, 911S ventilated disc)
Tire size, front & rear: 911T .... 165 HR 15
  911, 911S .... 185/70 VR 15
  911E (U.S. version) .... 185 HR 15
Wheels: 911, 911T, 911E .... Bolt-on steel disc
  911S .... Forged alloy
Body builder .... Porsche & Karmann

On the Targa, the rear window became a wraparound glass assembly to replace the zip-out soft rear section which was never completely satisfactory—leaky and noisy.

Significant changes were made to the engines of the 1969 cars; the T now had two Weber model 40 IDT carburetors, but the E and S were equipped with Bosch high-pressure mechanical fuel injection. The E, with 9:1 compression ratio, had 140 DIN horsepower at 6500 rpm, and the S, with 9.8:1, produced 170 at 6800. The Bosch pump was driven by a toothed belt from the left camshaft. Revs, throttle opening and fuel were monitored by a control system which operated a cam lobe in the injection pump. A centrifugal mechanism moved the cam axially as it was rotated by the throttle linkage.

Transmission options for the T and E models were four- or five-speed manual, or Sportomatic. Only the five-speed was available in the S.

An even bigger change in the 911 engine came with the C-series cars in September 1969, when the 1970 models went into production. A bore increase of four millimeters brought the displacement up to 2195 cc and along with that the horsepower increased by about the same percentage; and T, now with twin Zenith 40 TIN carburetors, went from 110 to 125 horsepower, the E from 140 to 155, and the S was up from 170 to 180—both of the latter with Bosch fuel injection. To handle the extra power, the Fichtel & Sachs clutch was enlarged from 215 to 225 mm.

Typically, handling was not ignored, and the front strut upper attachment points were moved forward 14 mm (0.55 inch) which lightened the steering effort and reduced kickback to the wheel.

The Boge self-leveling hydro-pneumatic front struts were phased out in 1971 as they weren't all that popular with buyers of the 911E (where the struts were standard) and were seldom ordered by buyers of the T or S versions.

Not much else of significance was done to the B- or C-series 911. As before, the cars underwent constant minor modifications and improvements as the Porsche engineers developed new ideas. And it may be unfair to say that there were no other significant changes because the myriad minor improvements made almost monthly by Porsche taken together all added up to a significantly improved automobile.

1972–1973

A further increase in engine displacement, for the 1972 911 series, was the big news for Porsche enthusiasts in the fall of 1971. The increase was accomplished by lengthening the stroke from 66 to 70.4 mm, while the bores remained at 84 mm. The cars were called 2.4s, but the actual displacement was 2341 cc. As before, the T, E and S versions were offered, all with slightly increased horsepower. The goal, though, in making the engine larger, was not more power to achieve more performance, but was to enable an emission-legal U.S. engine to have the torque and flexibility to result in good driveability.

Compression ratios were lower: The T was down to 7.5:1 from 8.6, the E was now 8:1 instead of 9:1, and the S ratio was lowered from 9.8 to 8.5:1. Horsepower was up fifteen in the T, to 140, and ten each on the E and S, to 165 and 190 respectively. All three ran on regular gas in the United States, and "two-star" petrol in Britain.

The T now came with Bosch mechanical fuel injection like the E and S, and with new cam timing and larger ports the torque peaks were at lower revs, contributing to the flexibility. A four-speed transmission was standard in all three versions, but the Sportomatic and five-speed were options. The latter now had a "standard" shift pattern with first and second in the same plane. Rear axle ratios were still 3.85:1 for the Sportomatic, and 4.428 with both manual transmissions. The British importer standardized the five-speed for the E and S models.

The oil tank for the dry-sump system was moved from the right rear wheel arch to a position between the right rear wheel and the door, with a filler flap similar to the one for gasoline on the left front fender. This lasted only a year (to the fall of 1972) because service station attendants too often put fuel into the oil tank with unfortunate results.

Boge shock absorbers were standard equipment in 1972, but Konis or Bilsteins were optional. The 911S was equipped with anti-

New in 1969 was the 911E, which replaced the 911L. The E model was equipped with Boge hydro-pneumatic, self-leveling front struts which eliminated the front torsion bars. *Porsche+Audi*

The 911 C series was introduced in September 1969 as 1970 models, and had engines that displaced 2195 cc. These cars carried a decal of an engine silhouette with 2.2 superimposed on it in the back window of each car, as on this 1970 911T coupe. *Porsche+Audi*

roll bars of 15 mm diameter, front and rear. To further aid handling, the higher-powered S had an air dam under the front bumper which came about as a result of aerodynamic work by Porsche engineers. Front end lift was reduced from 183 to 102 pounds at 140 mph. This "chin spoiler" as it was sometimes called, was optional on the T and E, and the demand was so great it was made standard on all three versions.

The dry-sump oil tank was now made of stainless steel, and the fuel tank became larger (eighty-liter capacity) by stamping the upper half to fit the space-saver spare tire. Unfortunately, this type of spare is illegal in Britain because the law prohibits mounting a bias-ply tire on the same axle as a radial tire. Porsche provided a plastic bag into which the driver could put the road wheel with its flat tire, because the full-size tire (which would be dirty and smell bad after the car was brought to a stop with a flat tire) could not be put into the space normally occupied by the space-saver spare in the luggage compartment—it would have to be carried inside.

Chassis design and dimensions of the 1972–73 911 were almost identical to the '69, '70 and '71 but the wheelbase was once again lengthened, by a mere three millimeters, to 2,271 mm.

In late 1972, the Carrera name returned to a Porsche model for the first time since 1967 (the 906 Carrera Six). The 911RS, as it was called officially, used the body shell of the 911S, but was lightened in almost every way possible. It had no sound insulation, thinner body sheet metal, fiberglass rear lid, thinner windshield glass, no rear seats, and the two front seats were mere shells with thin padding, and every nonessential amenity was left off. The Carrera RS was meant for competition and had no emission equipment on it, so it couldn't be sold in the United States for road use.

These lightweight RS Carreras weighed in at under 2,000 pounds, and to give them added push, the engines were enlarged to 2687 cc. The stroke remained at 70.4 mm, as in the 1972–73 911, but the bore was increased from 84 to 90 mm. Because the Biral cylinders couldn't be bored to more than 87.5 mm (which would put it too near the

The Targa body style, shown here on a 1970 911S, was introduced in 1965, and has always been one of the more popular models. The first cars had zip-out back windows like those of normal convertibles, but problems caused Porsche to go to a fixed, glass rear window— maybe not quite as sporty, but eminently more practical. *Porsche+Audi*

As before. the 1970 911 could be ordered with either steel wheels, or the Fuchs five-spoke alloy wheels, as on this S coupe. *Porsche+Audi*

In 1971, the 911 was still available with either Coupe or Targa body, four- or five-speed all-synchromesh or three-speed Sportomatic trans- missions, and with T, E or S engine tune. This is the T, with optional sunroof and ten-spoke alloy wheels. *Porsche+Audi*

limit) the Biral cylinder liners were eliminated and the aluminum cylinder walls were coated with Nikasil, which is made up of nickel and silicon carbide. The result was a reduction in both friction and wear. Bosch timed injection was used on the Carrera as well as the T and E and, with 8.5:1 compression ratio, the Carrera's power was 210 DIN/230 SAE at 6300 rpm.

Original plans called for 500 Carreras to be produced to qualify the RS in the Group 4 Special GT category, but approximately 1,600 of this version were built during the 1973 model year. The reason for the higher production figure was that the Carrera could be used on the road in Europe, and enthusiast drivers took advantage of the opportunity. Of the total production, 1,036 were stripped lightweights, and around 600 were trimmed as per 911S specifications.

In order to get and keep the extra power on the road, the rear wheel rims were widened to seven inches (the fronts remained at six inches, as on the 911S), and the front air dam was augmented by a "ducktail" spoiler mounted on the rear fiberglass engine compartment lid. The rear spoiler reduced rear-end lift from 320 to ninety-three pounds at top speed, and moved the aerodynamic center of pressure about six inches to the rear, which helped high-speed stability in cross winds.

Peter Gregg won both the Trans-Am and IMSA championships in 1973 with a Carrera RSR, which was a further modification of the RS (the RSR had a displacement of 2806 cc, and 300-plus horsepower), and the model won outright victory in the Targa Florio, in Sicily.

1974

Throughout the years Porsche had made running changes, in addition to the annual model changes, to improve its cars. Speed, both acceleration and top, was always sought-after, but flexibility and ease of driving were just as important—maybe more so. Speed for speed's sake isn't that difficult to achieve; but speed coupled with a flexible engine is the ultimate goal.

Factory engineers know, just as hot rodders do, that bigger-is-better (or, when in doubt get out the boring bar). Unlike hot rodders though, factory engineers have other things to consider—like manufacturing economy, and reliability of the car when driven by a large number and variety of customers.

So, after only two years of the 2.4-liter Porsches, the 1974 911 and 911S (the T and E designations were dropped) displayed at the 1973 Frankfurt auto show had larger engines. Matching the Carrera, which continued from 1973, all 911 series cars now had a bore of 90 mm and a stroke of 70.4 mm resulting in 2687 cc displacement. Further standardizing the model, Bosch CIS (Continuous Injection System) fuel injection, introduced in mid-1973 on the 2.4-liter T model, was used on all 911 models, regardless of the state of tune.

The standard transmission for all models sold in the United States was the four-speed manual-shift unit (the five-speed was standard in England), with five-speed manual and four-speed Sportomatic optional. Rear axle ratios were 3.857:1 for Sportomatic-equipped cars, and 4.429:1 for manual-transmission cars.

Horsepower was actually reduced a bit in the 1974 Porsches; the 911 was rated at 150 DIN/143 SAE at 5700 and both the 911S and Carrera had 175 DIN/167 SAE at 5800 rpm. But, because of better torque characteristics, and continual improvements in chassis and suspension, the 1974 911 series was the finest and most enjoyable-to-drive Porsche to date.

To meet ever-increasing U.S. safety regulations, heavy-duty aluminum bumpers, front and rear, were incorporated into the design. The bumpers projected several inches from the bodywork and were attached by collapsible aluminum alloy tubes that crushed under severe impact—protecting the body—but had to be replaced after each incident. A hydraulic shock-absorbing attachment that didn't have to be replaced was standard on U.K. cars and optional in other markets. Accordion-pleated rubber boots covered the gap between bumpers and body, and the overall result was one of the better adaptations of safety bumpers to an existing body (in this case, one that had been in production for more than ten years). Other car companies, particularly some of those in Europe, should take note.

Underneath, a 16 mm front anti-roll bar was standard on the 911 and 911S, while the Carrera carried a 20 mm front bar. Forged aluminum alloy rear trailing arms, with large wheel bearings, replaced the welded steel arms of previous models.

Inside, there were a redesigned steering wheel with extra padding, new instrument panel knobs, higher-backed lightweight seats with inertia-reel belt/harness and an electronic tachometer. The Carrera was also given the electric window lifts which had been optional on all 911 models, but were now standard on the Carrera.

Outside, visual identification in addition to the safety bumpers were the front air dam, or chin spoiler, which was now standard on all versions; a new tail-pipe/muffler arrangement because of the new bumpers; large rubber "cushions" on the rear bumpers, and rear fender flairs. On the Carrera, which was now legal for road use in the United States, the ducktail spoiler was still on the rear engine lid and large script lettering on the lower body sides identified the model as a Carrera in case anyone was in doubt. The 911, 911S and Carrera were

available in both coupe and Targa body styles.

While the "2.7-liter" engine for the production 911 series seemed adequate, a further step was taken for competition when Porsche built the RSR version in 1974. Designed as a customer racer, with a planned production of 100 units to satisfy FIA homologation requirements, the RSR had a full three liters displacement, obtained by combining a 95 mm bore with the existing 70.4 mm stroke; the result being 2993 cc. The crankcase was made of aluminum rather than magnesium as before.

Because the FIA requirements dictate a "road" car rather than "race" car, these RSR models could be, and were, used by customers on the road (in Europe at least, as they weren't U.S. road-legal) as well as on the track. Out of a total production of 109 vehicles, only forty-nine were stripped racers, while the other sixty carried at least some passenger amenities. The RS version was rated at 230 horsepower, and the RSR at 315 initially, but a switch from throttle butterflies to slide valve throttle opening brought power up to 330 at 8000 rpm.

The RSR was not raced by the factory in either 1974 or 1975, but private entrants

---

911T, 911E, 911S (1969-71) changes
Engine
Design: . . . . Air-cooled, flat (opposed) six
Borexstroke, mm/inches: 1969 . . . . 80x66/3.15x2.60
 1970-71 . . . . 84x66/3.31x2.60
Displacement, cc/cubic inches: 1969 . . . . 1991/121.5
 1970-71 . . . . 2195/133.8
Valve operation: Chain-driven single overhead camshaft on each bank with rocker arms & inclined valves
Compression ratio: 911T 8.6:1
 911E 9.1:1
 911S 1969 . . . . 9.9:1
 911S 1970-71 . . . . 9.8:1
Carburetion: 911T 1969 . . . . Two Weber 40 IDT
 911T 1970-71 . . . . Two Zenith 40 TIN
 911E, 911S . . . . Bosch timed fuel injection
BHP (Mfr): 911T 1969 . . . . 110 DIN/125 SAE @ 5800
 911T 1970-71 . . . . 125 DIN/145 SAE @ 5800
 911E 1969 . . . . 140 DIN/160 SAE @ 6500
 911E 1970-71 . . . . 155 DIN/175 SAE @ 6200
 911S 1969 . . . . 170 DIN/190 SAE @ 6800
 911S 1970-71 . . . . 180 DIN/200 SAE @ 6500
Chassis & drivetrain
Transmission: 911T, 911E . . . . Four- or five-speed all-synchromesh, or Sportomatic

911S . . . . Porsche five-speed, all-synchromesh
Axle ratio: 911T, 911E (Sportomatic) 3.86:1
 911T, 911E (with standard four-speed, or 911S five-speed)
 . . . . 4.43:1
 911T, 911E, 911S (optional ratios with four- or five-speed)
 . . . . 4.833 or 4.38:1
Rear suspension: . . Independent, semi-trailing link on each side with transverse torsion bars & telescopic shock absorbers (anti-roll bar standard on 911S, optional on T & E)
Front suspension: 911T, 911S . . . . . . Independent, MacPherson telescopic shock strut and triangulated wishbone on each side, with longitudinal torsion bars & anti-roll bar
 911E . . . . Boge hydro-pneumatic gas/oil shock strut & triangulated wishbone on each side & anti-roll bar
General
Wheelbase, mm/inches: 2268/89.3
Track, front, mm/inches: 1374/54.1
 rear, mm/inches: 1355/53.3
Brakes: . . . . Ate disc
Tire size, front & rear: 911T . . . . 165 HR 15
 911S . . . . 185/70 VR 15
 911E (U.S. version) . . . . 185 HR 14
Wheels: 911T, 911E . . . . Bolt-on steel disc
 911S . . . . Pressure-cast alloy
Body builder: . . . . Porsche

upheld the marque's honor everywhere Porsches were raced.

Another addition for 1974, appreciated mainly by those who actually drove their Porsches in the winter (skiers mostly), was the headlight washers. Because some form of on-board automatic headlight washer is required in Sweden, which is a good Porsche market, Porsche engineers experimented with wash and wipe, using water jets and miniature wipers like those on the windshield, and with straight jets of water without wipers—which they finally settled on. A nine-quart reservoir, which was filled through a "neck" beside the fuel filler in the left front fender, supplied water to the high-pressure jets mounted in front of each headlight on the front bumper.

1975

Changes for the 1975 model were minimal: The heating system, long a bane of Porsche owners, was improved both in amount and control of hot air, with the driver and passenger able to control each side individually. Alternators were upgraded to handle the load of a variety of electrical equipment that was either standard or optional, including electric windows, sun-

roof, rear window de-mister and the heater fan itself.

Running changes continued to be made as the factory engineers juggled transmission gear ratios to meet changing driving conditions caused by safety and emission regulations from all over the world. Once again a single battery, located at the front of the luggage compartment, was used.

1976

More significant changes were made to the 1976 911 line. After battling the rust and corrosion problem for many years, as has every other car builder in the world, Porsche adopted use of a zinc coating to each side of the car's sheet metal (both chassis and body) which allowed the company to issue a six-year no-rust warranty.

The heater system was once again improved by the addition of a temperature control unit where the driver set a dial on a number between one and ten, to suit his preference, and two sensors, one inside the car and one in the left heater hose, maintained that temperature. Also, for the first time on a Porsche, a cruise control was offered. This was aimed at the American market where such a device has great value on long stretches of interstate highway;

The interior of the 1972 911 models continued the tradition of comfortable elegance. Three transmissions (four- or five-speed manual or three-speed Sportomatic) were offered. *Porsche+Audi*

reducing driving fatigue, improving mileage, and very likely reducing the probability of brushes with the law (assuming, of course, that the driver doesn't set the cruise speed at 100).

The American market had two Porsches available in 1976, the 3.0 Turbo and the 911S 2.7. The S had most of the equipment (standard) seen on the previous year's Carrera; tinted glass, two-speed plus intermittent windshield wipers, two-stage rear window heating, front and rear anti-roll bars and five-speed transmission. Options included Koni adjustable or Bilstein gas/oil shock absorbers, external oil cooler (located in right front fender), forged alloy wheels, sport seats, electric sunroof, electric windows and air conditioning. Standard transmission was the four-speed manual in most markets, but the U.K. and American distributors specified the five-speed as standard.

Some 2.7s, which were hot-running cars, had trouble with cylinder studs pulling out of the crankcase.

1977

Few changes were made for 1977, as the 911 series cars were nearing perfection insofar as the basic concept would permit.

911T, 911E, 911S, Carrera 2.7 (1972, 73) changes

Engine

Design: . . . . Air-cooled, flat (opposed) six
Borexstroke, mm/inches: 911T, E, S 84x70.4/3.31x2.77
   Carrera (1973 only)* 90x70.4/3.54x2.77
Displacement, cc/cubic inches: 911T, E, S 2341/142.8
   Carrera 2687/163.9
Valve operation: Chain-driven single overhead camshaft on each bank with rocker arms & inclined valves
Compression ratio: 911T (to mid-1973 model year) 7.5:1
   911T (from mid-1973 model year) 8:1
   911E 8:1
   911S, Carrera 8.5:1
Carburetion: 911T (to mid-1973 model year) . . . . Two Zenith 40
   911T (from mid-1973 model year) . . Bosch CIS fuel injection
   911E, 911S, Carrera . . . . Bosch timed fuel injection
BHP (Mfr): 911T (to mid-1973 model year) . . . . 130 DIN/150 SAE @5600
   911T (from mid-1973 model year) . . . . 140 DIN/157 SAE @ 5600
   911E . . . . 165 DIN/185 SAE @ 6200
   911S . . . . 190 DIN/210 SAE @ 6500
   Carrera 2.7 . . . . 210 DIN/230 SAE @ 6300
* The 911 Carrera 2.7 was introduced in 1973 for track use only in the U.S. but could be used on the road in Europe.

Chassis & drivetrain

Transmission: . . . . . Four-speed, all-synchromesh (five-speed or Sportomatic optional)
Axle ratio: . . . . 3.87 or 4.43:1
Rear suspension: . . . . . . Independent, semi-trailing link on each side with transverse torsion bars, telescopic shock absorbers & anti-roll bar
Front suspension: . . . . Independent, MacPherson telescopic shock strut and triangulated wishbone on each side, with longitudinal torsion bars & anti-roll bar

General

Wheelbase, mm/inches: 2271/89.4
Track, front, mm/inches: 911T 1360/53.5
   911E, 911S, Carrera 2.7 . . . . 1372/54.0
   rear, mm/inches: 911T 1342/52.8
   911E, 911S 1354/53.3
   Carrera 2.7 . . . . 1394/54.8
Tire size, front & rear: . . . . 185/70 VR 15
Wheels: . . . . Pressure-cast alloy
Body builder: . . . . Porsche

In 1972, displacement was increased to 2341 cc, and the cars carried 2.4 lettering on the rear air intake as on this 911T. The oil filler for the dry-sump tank was under the cap just below the right rear quarter window. This lasted only for 1972, as too many cars had gasoline put into the oil filler by careless gas station attendants. Decals along the rear of the engine compartment told the owner everything from tire pressures to valve clearances. *Porsche+Audi*

More transmission-ratio juggling took place, and the interior door locks were changed, with shorter buttons and knurled knobs set into the door lining—all as an attempt to thwart thieves. Porsches rank with Corvettes as the most stolen cars in the world, so it would take much more than that to secure one, but I suppose it would slow down the amateur a bit.

The Sportomatic-equipped cars received a brake servo booster for the markets that bought left-hand-drive cars (a year later all

The 911S for 1972 came equipped with a front "air dam" or "spoiler" which reduced front end lift from 183 to 102 pounds at 140 mph—the top speed of the S. The spoiler was optional on the T and E, and became so popular that it was made standard equipment on all three models later in 1972. This car has European Quartz Iodine lights (which can be installed on any 911/912). Below are the typical U.S.-style sealed-beam units. *Porsche+Audi*

In 1973, some new alloy wheels became available, called "cookie cutters" by the press and Porsche enthusiasts. *Porsche+Audi*

Porsches were so equipped), which seemed mainly to help when the brakes were cold, and at lower speeds.

The 1977 models, then, had running detail improvements that had become a Porsche hallmark, but were void of any significant changes. In the fall of 1977, when the 1978 models were introduced, Porsche made another big change in the 911 series cars: Only two 911 types were available—the three-liter SC and the 3.3-liter Turbo.

1978

The SC was virtually a Carrera without the name, as it had the same mechanical specifications, flared wheel openings and the wider wheels. Horsepower was down to 180 from the Carrera's 200, but a higher and flatter torque curve made the car much more enjoyable to drive. A new, stronger crankshaft with larger bearings was used, and the crankcase was once again aluminum (it had been aluminum through the 1967 911 cars, then from the 1968 through 1977 it was pressure-cast magnesium). An air pump, to meet emission requirements, was made standard for all Porsche markets, and a breakerless CD distributor was adopted across the board.

1979–1982

A new clutch disc hub for the five-speed manual transmission eliminated gear chatter at low speeds, and servo-assisted brakes were now standard. The 1979 911SC would continue with the same specifications as the 1978 version, but the Sportomatic transmission was phased out of production.

A two-millimeter bore increase, to 97 mm, and a stroke increase of four millimeters, to 74.4, gave the 930 Turbo a displacement of 3299 cc, the largest and most powerful production Porsche engine to date. With a 7:1 compression ratio, the Turbo produced 300 DIN horsepower at 5500 rpm, and 303 pounds-feet of torque at 4000 rpm. An air-to-air intercooler was squeezed into the engine compartment, which necessitated moving the air-conditioning condensor to the right side of the air-intake grille on the spoiler.

To cope with the added performance, in 1978 the 930 Turbo received the vented and cross-drilled brake discs and four-piston calipers of the 917. Performance of the 3.3 Turbo was and is sensational, and in tests conducted by *Motor* magazine, in England, the car went from 0–60 in 5.3 seconds, 0–100 in 12.3 seconds, and 0–120 mph in 19.1 seconds. In braking tests, *Motor* staffers found that the 930 would stop in 174 feet from 70 mph, and there was no brake fade evident in twenty successive stops (at forty-five-second intervals) from 100 mph.

When the new clutch disc hub was introduced in 1978, its larger size caused the engine to be mounted farther toward the rear of the car by 30 mm (1.18 inches) and even though no handling difference was

The Carrera name returned to the Porsche line in 1973 on the 911RS (for Rennsport, or race sport). It had a 2687 cc engine, no sound insulation, thinner sheet metal and glass, fiberglass rear lid with a small ducktail spoiler, and no emission equipment so it couldn't be sold for road use in the United States (it was raced in the United States, however). It was popular as a road car in Europe. *Porsche+Audi*

The 1973 911T Targa with the top on showed how open-air motoring could be done in relative safety, as the Targa "T-handle" was also a roll-over bar. Options included choice of three engines, three transmissions and forged-alloy wheels. The bumpers were made stronger for 1973. *Porsche+Audi*

Visually, the 1974 911 models could be identified by the heavier side strip below the doors, and the U.S.-required "safety" bumpers. To Porsche's credit, the adoption of the mandatory bumpers was accomplished better than on any other make, as they blended well into the existing body forms. Underneath, the engine was enlarged once more, this time to the 2687 cc of the previous year's Carrera. All three 1974 models—911, 911S and Carrera—had the same displacement. The horsepower rating was 150 DIN/143 SAE for the 911; 175 DIN/167 SAE for the S and Carrera. *Porsche+Audi*

The 911 Carrera was made available to the American buyer for street use in 1974; and other than the bumpers and side trim, was visually much like the 1973 Carrera. This is one of the most sought-after Porsches. *Porsche+Audi*

discernible in any but racetrack conditions, Porsche engineers called for the rear tire pressure to be increased from thirty-four to forty-three pounds per square inch.

Since 1978, all changes to the 911SC have been the typically Porsche improvements by degree, and it is likely both that this practice will continue, and that no new major changes will occur. It isn't impossible, of course—Porsche management has surprised us before, but it is unlikely.

At the Geneva auto show in March 1982, a true convertible 911SC joined the Coupe and Targa body styles. While many Porsche owners or enthusiasts couldn't care less about a convertible, the body style may well keep the 911 series in production longer than would be otherwise practical. This was assuming, which was dangerous to do with

Porsche, that neither the 944 or 928 would become available as a convertible.

In the event that a convertible was added to one or both of the front-engined water-cooled Porsche lines, it would only affect 911 convertible sales to a very minor degree in my opinion. Too many Porsche enthusiasts saw the 911SC as the last *real* Porsche, and the water-cooled models as "some other kind of car." This view probably wasn't shared by those new to the Porsche ranks who didn't know or care about the "tradition."

Regardless, the 911SC is a great automobile—the best of the traditional Porsches, and the one to buy if you like driving for the sheer pleasure of driving. It takes a better-than-average driver to get the most from the 911, which is a big reason why 911 owners feel superior to other Porsche drivers, and don't even consider drivers of other makes as *drivers*. The 911 owners are proud of their cars, and proud of themselves (sometimes to absurdity) for their intelligence in selecting this superior means of transportation.

1983

So far, the talk of adding a convertible to the 928 or 924/944 body styles was just that, talk. Rumor. I still wouldn't bet against it, but for the 1983 the 911SC Cabriolet was the only fully open car in the Porsche line. The 911SC Coupe and Targa continued as well, and still got minor improvements as Porsche engineering saw fit.

1984

At the 1983 Frankfurt auto show, where the 1984 models were shown, the SC became the Carrera—a name that had started in

---

911, 911S, Carrera, Carrera RS & RSR (1974) changes

Engine

Design: .... Air-cooled, flat (opposed) six

Borexstroke, mm/inches: 911, 911S, Carrera 90x70.4/3.54x2.77

Carrera RS, RSR 95x70.4/3.77x2.77

Displacement, cc/cubic inches: 911, 911S, Carrera 2687/163.97

Carrera RS, RSR 2993/182.57

Valve operation: Chain-driven single overhead camshaft on each bank with rocker arms & inclined valves

Compression ratio: 911 .... 8:1

911S, 911 Carrera, Carrera RS, RSR 8.5:1

Carburetion: .... Bosch CIS timed fuel injection

BHP (Mfr*): 911 .... 150 DIN/143 SAE @ 5700

911S, Carrera .... 175 DIN/167 SAE @ 5800

Carrera RS .... 230 DIN/220 SAE @ 6500

Carrera RSR .... 330 DIN/320 SAE @ 8000

Chassis & drivetrain

Axle ratio: with four- or five-speed 4.429:1

with Sportomatic 3.857:1

Rear suspension: .. Independent, semi-trailing link on each side with transverse torsion bars, telescopic shock absorbers (& anti-roll bar on Carrera)

Front suspension: .... Independent, MacPherson telescopic shock strut and triangulated wishbone on each side, with longitudinal torsion bars & anti-roll bar

General

Wheelbase, mm/inches: 2271/89.4

Track, front, mm/inches: 911 (with 5½J–15 wheel) 1360/53.5

911S, Carrera (with 6-15 wheel) 1372/54.0

rear, mm/inches: 911 (with 5½J–15 wheel) 1342/52.8

911S, Carrera (with 6-15 wheel) 1354/53.3

Carrera (with 7J wheel) 1380/54.3

Tire size, front & rear: 911 .... 165 HR 15

911S .... 185/70 VR 15

Carrera .... 185/70 VR 15 front & 215/60 VR 15 rear

Body builder: .... Porsche

*Note: In 1973 the SAE (Society of Automotive Engineers) changed its horsepower rating system, using net instead of gross power so, for the first time, SAE ratings were lower than DIN (Deutsche Industrie Normal) ratings from 1974 on.

Porsche is one of the few companies that has been successful in convincing buyers that cloth upholstery is as good as, and in some cases better than, leather—particularly on either very hot or very cold days. This is a 1974 911 interior. *Porsche+Audi*

1953 and was abandoned in 1965, revived again in 1972 and dropped again in 1977, and once again appeared on the 911 Carrera for 1984. Engine size was increased to 3164 cc by using the 74.4 mm stroke crankshaft of the Turbo with the 95 mm bore of the SC. The Bosch K-Jetronic injection was replaced with the DME (Digital Motor Electronic) "Motronic" injection and ignition system. Power was increased to 200 SAE at 5900 rpm.

To cope with the added horsepower, the brake discs were made 3.5 mm thicker with larger ventilation passages, and the balance control from the 928S was utilized to help prevent front wheel lockup under severe braking. Leather upholstery was standard on the Carrera. A five-speed transmission was the buyer's only choice, but Coupe, Targa or Cabriolet body styles were available. The 911 Turbo Coupe also continued, virtually unchanged and with only a four-speed manual transmission. These were the choices of the air-cooled, rear-engined-Porsche buyer in 1984 and 1985, but the Turbo was still available only in Europe.

1985

By 1985, Porsche had built more than 200,000 of the 911 series in its various forms. As before, small changes that might be considered insignificant in themselves (but when added up made a considerable difference in the car over the years) continued to be made. Considering that the 911 design was twenty years old (from a marketing standpoint, but several years older considering conception and development time), the 911 series had evolved into a car that was not yet at its peak of development.

Few had thought the model would last this long, but it did—and continued to get better. Almost any option one could want, except an automatic transmission, was available on a 911 Carrera, and it is doubtful if the lack of an automatic has harmed sales.

1986

The 911 Turbo Coupe once again became available in the United States as a street-legal car, but the "Americanization" of the four-wheel-drive 959 was abandoned because "Americanization would destroy it." There was doubt that the engine could ever conform to U.S. emission regulations; to meet U.S. bumper height, a total redesign of thirty percent of the body structures would have been required. Even if it could be made to meet U.S. requirements the cost for conversion (for the limited number to be produced) would have been astronomical. The 959 was therefore built only for European road use, and for U.S. track use.

Warranty coverage was extended for 1986, with vehicle coverage for two years and unlimited mileage (1985 carried it for one

In 1975, the Carrera got what is now referred to as the "whale-tail" rear spoiler. This device was designed by Porsche for the 930 Turbo and 935 race cars so it had plenty of development before application to the Carrera. *Porsche+Audi*

year and unlimited mileage), five years or 50,000 miles on the power train, and ten years on rust perforation (up from seven years).

As before, the 911 Carrera and 911 Turbo were available worldwide—the Carrera in Coupe, Targa and Cabriolet body styles; the Turbo in Coupe only.

1987

The 1987 911 Carrera and 911 Turbo had little change, but horsepower was up from 200 to 214 for the Carrera. A new clutch, hydraulically assisted, and a new five-speed transmission helped the car achieve 149 mph top speed and 0–60 in 6.1 seconds. The 911 Turbo produced 282 bhp with a top speed of 157 and 0–60 in 5.5 seconds.

New colors were added, as well as additional leather trim options, and new electrically adjustable seats had additional lumbar support. All of which added up to better cars, with a higher price; the 911 Carrera Coupe at $38,500, the Targa at $40,500, the Cabriolet at $44,500, and the Turbo Coupe at $58,750.

In March 1987, a slant-nose "935 look," called the 930S, became an option for the 911 Turbo—for $23,244 extra. The sloping nose included retractable headlights, functional air outlet vents behind the lights, and air scoops in front of the rear wheels for additional engine and brake cooling. The 930S package was available on Coupe, Targa, and Cabriolet models.

1988

The 911 Carrera name continued for 1988, in Coupe, Cabriolet, and Targa body styles; still with 3164 cc displacement and 214 hp. The 11 Turbo and 930S, also in all three body configurations, was also to continue and it retained its 3299 cc and 282 hp flat-six engine.

The 1975 911 silver anniversary edition had silver cloth in seats and doors to complement the black leather trim and black carpeting. *Porsche+Audi*

911, 911S, 911S/C, Carrera, Turbo (1975) changes	
Engine	
Design: . . . . Air-cooled, flat (opposed) six	
Borexstroke, mm/inches: 911, 911S, Carrera,	
911S/C (U.S.) 90x70.4/3.54x2.77	
Turbo 95x70.4/3.74x2.77	
Displacement, cc/cubic inches: 911, 911S, Carrera,	
911S/C 2687/163.97	
Turbo 2993/182.70	
Compression ratio: 911 . . . . 8:1	
911S, Carrera, 911S/C 8.5:1	
Turbo 6.5:1	
Valve operation: Chain-driven single overhead camshaft on each bank with rocker arms & inclined valves	
Carburetion: . . . . Bosch K-Jetronic fuel injection	
BHP (Mfr): 911 . . . . 150 DIN/143 SAE @ 5700	
911S . . . . 175 DIN/167 SAE @ 5800	
Carrera . . . . 210 DIN/200 SAE @ 6300	
911S/C (U.S.) . . . . 165 DIN/157 SAE @ 5800	
Turbo . . . . 260 DIN/248 SAE @ 5500	

Chassis & drivetrain
Axle ratio: 3.87:1
Rear suspension: . . . . . . Independent, semi-trailing link on each side with transverse torsion bars & telescopic shock absorbers & anti-roll bar
Front suspension: . . . . Independent, MacPherson telescopic shock strut and triangulated wishbone on each side, with longitudinal torsion bars & anti-roll bar
General
Wheelbase, mm/inches: 911, 911S, Carrera, 911S/C 2271/89.4
Turbo 2272/89.4
Track, front, mm/inches: 911, 911S, Carrera,
911S/C 1372/54.0
Turbo 1438/56.6
rear, mm/inches: 911, 911S 1354/53.3
Carrera 1380/54.3
Turbo 1511/59.5
911S/C . . . . . . (depending on wheels) 1342 or 1368/52.8–53.8
Tire size, front & rear: 911 Turbo . . . . 185/70 VR 15 & 215/60 VR 15

There were few mechanical or body changes, none of them major, for the 1988 911 series cars although Porsche, as usual, continued to add safety and comfort convenience features to all its cars.

In honor of the twenty-fifth anniversary of the 911, a Silver Anniversary model, with diamond blue metallic paint and body-colored

The detachable Targa (this is a 1975 911S) top section could be stowed in the front luggage compartment. A soft top could also be ordered as an option, which stowed in a smaller area leaving more space for luggage. The Carrera was also available as a Targa. *Porsche+Audi*

While the basic body shell of the 911 didn't change much after 1965, the engine compartment kept getting more added to it. This is a 1976 911S engine. *Porsche+Audi*

911, Carrera 3.0, Turbo, Turbo Carrera (1976–77) changes

Engine
Design: .... Air-cooled, flat (opposed) six
Borexstroke, mm/inches: 911 .... 90x70.4/3.54x2.77
  Carrera 3.0, Turbo, Turbo Carrera (U.S.) 95x70.4/3.74x2.77
Displacement, cc/cubic inches: 911 .... 2687/163.90
  Carrera 3.0, Turbo, Turbo Carrera 2993/182.57
Valve operation: Chain-driven single overhead camshaft on each bank with rocker arms & inclined valves
Compression ratio: 911, Carrera 3.0 .... 8.5:1
  Turbo, Turbo Carrera 6.5:1
Carburetion: 911, Carrera 3.0 ... Bosch K-Jetronic fuel injection
  Turbo, Turbo Carrera .... KKK Turbocharger & Bosch K-Jetronic fuel injection
BHP (Mfr): 911 .... 165 DIN/157 SAE @ 5800
  Carrera 3.0 .... 200 DIN/191 SAE @ 6000
  Turbo .... 260 DIN/248 SAE @ 5500
  Turbo (U.S. & Japan) .... 245 DIN/234 SAE @ 5500
General
Wheelbase, mm/inches: 2272/89.4
Track, front, mm/inches: 911, Carrera 3.0 .... 1369/53.9
  Turbo, Turbo Carrera 1438/56.6
  rear, mm/inches: 911 .... 1354/53.3
  Carrera 3.0 .... 1380/54.3
  Turbo, Turbo Carrera 1511/59.5
Body builder: .... Porsche

The 1976 Turbo Carrera (Turbo, in Europe) had a larger rear spoiler with two intake vents; one for the engine and one for the air-conditioning condenser. The front wheel openings were flared to accommodate the extra-wide VR high-speed radial tires. The turbocharged, CIS-injected engine developed 234 hp and, driving through a four-speed transmission, gave the Turbo Carrera a top speed of 155 mph, even with U.S. emission equipment. *Porsche+Audi*

The Turbo Carrera was continued in 1977, with no discernible visual difference from 1976. The standard Turbo Carrera was fully equipped, including air conditioning, stereo, leather interior and power windows. *Porsche+Audi*

By 1976, all 911 series cars were beginning to look alike, with few and very minor visual differences from year to year. The outside rearview mirror is the only visual difference from 1975. This is a 1976 911S. *Porsche+Audi*

The 1978 911SC, with more flare to the rear wheel openings but otherwise looking like Porsches of the previous few years, boasted more creature comforts and conveniences. The outside rearview mirrors were electrically adjusted and heated, and the door locks supposedly made the car theft-proof. Unfortunately, it has been proven that if a thief wants the Porsche badly enough, there isn't much to stop him short of an armed guard. *Porsche+ Audi*

wheels, and silver blue leather interior with "F. Porsche" signature on the head restraint was built in a run of 300 cars. Production was divided between the three body styles and the MSRP was $45,200 for the Coupe, $47,485 for the Targa, and $52,050 for the Cabriolet.

1989

Three new models—actually two variations on the 911 theme, the 911 Club Sport and 911 Speedster, and the all-new 911 Carrera 4—were introduced in the 1989 model year.

The Club Sport was simply a lightened cafe racer. (By eliminating A/C, power windows and power door locks, radio, sound insulation, fog lights, front hood lock, door armrests, and rear seat the Club Sport weighed 155 pounds less than a stock 911 Carrera Coupe.) The 3.2-liter engine, still rated at 214 hp, had Digital Motor Electronics control system and hollow intake valves, the combination increasing maxi-

The large rear spoiler with two air intakes introduced in 1976 was replaced by one of a different shape and configuration for 1978; it had one intake area with forward-facing louvers and more of a "tray" around the edge of the spoiler. *Author*

The interior of the 930 Turbo looked much like the 911SC in its most deluxe form, except that the Turbo only came with a four-speed transmission and the 911SC had five speeds. The Turbo also had a 7000 rpm tach, red-lined at 6800, while the SC had an 8000 rpm tach red-lined at 6400 rpm.

The 930 engine compartment got more crowded as it had to accommodate the air-conditioning condenser and compressor.

mum engine speed to 6840 rpm instead of the 6520 of the 911 Carrera.

Because of the minimal engine changes, acceleration was increased so that the Club Sport could do 0–60 in 5.6 seconds and had a top speed of 149 mph. MSRP was $45,895.

The 911 Carrera Speedster became available in January 1989 and was based on the Carrera Cabriolet. The Speedster windshield, framed in aluminum, was raked five more degrees than the Cabriolet, and the top (like the 356 Speedster) was unlined. The 930S slant-nose body style was available as an option.

Four-wheel drive in an affordable Porsche was the really big news for 1989 when the Carrera 4 was introduced as a coupe only.

The 1980 911SC "Weissach Coupe" limited edition had the appearance of the Turbo but without the Turbo's engine. *Porsche+Audi*

Nineteen years after the 901 was first shown to the public, the basic body shell was unchanged; the wheel openings were flared, the bumpers protruded farther out from the body, and several styles of alloy wheels were available with fatter tires, but the total look was not unlike 1963—which is just fine with me. *Author*

Powered by a 3.6–liter sohc flat-six air-cooled engine with twin plug ignition which put out 247 hp at 6100 rpm, the "4" would accelerate from 0–60 in 5.7 seconds and attain 162 mph top speed.

This was the most sophisticated road Porsche since the 959 but, at $69,500, the Carrera 4 was considerably more affordable than the 959 at $200,000.

The Carrera 4's four-wheel-drive system is full time, and the center differential splits the torque thirty-one percent to the front wheels, fifty-nine percent to the rear; however, computer-controlled multiple-disc clutches in the center and rear differentials apportion power to each wheel in the maximum amount it will accept without spinning.

For the first time since the 911 was introduced, in 1963, the chassis (floor pan and suspension) was completely new. Coil springs replace torsion bars all around, and the front suspension consists of MacPherson struts with lower control arms while the rear suspension has semi-trailing arms.

An early 911 6J–15 Fuchs forged-aluminum oem wheel. All factory-installed Fuchs wheels are forged, but some aftermarket suppliers offer cast-alloy Fuchs copies. Forged wheels are safer because, on impact, they will bend rather than fracture. *Author*

The late 911 6J–15 alloy oem wheel was similar to the early wheel, but with blacked-out spokes. It was also a forged wheel. *Author*

The 911E and 914/6 used this 5½J–14 single-piece, forged-alloy wheel as oem equipment. Aside from appearance, the main advantage of an alloy wheel is light weight and more precise tolerances (lateral and vertical runout—concentricity between hub and rim). *Author*

The 1967 911S 4½J–15 one-piece, forged-alloy wheel, by Fuchs. This style, but wider (5½-, 6- or 7-inch) has now become popular on any model Porsche that has the right bolt circle. *Author*

"Cookie cutter" pressure-cast alloy wheel by ATS comes in 15x6- or 7-inch rim widths. This wheel has also been used on 911s and 944s. *Author*

The rear spoiler, which lies flush with the rear deck while at rest, raises automatically at about 40 mph, lowering (again, automatically) at about six mph.

While the 911 Carrera 4 looks a lot like previous 911 models, there are virtually no mechanical and few body parts that are interchangeable.

Early driving impressions indicate that this is the very best handling customer road car ever built by Porsche, and it will undoubtedly point the way for manufacturers of high-performance road cars. The combination of maximum traction for acceleration and for less-than-perfect roads, and the Bosch Anti-Lock Braking System also make the 911 Carrera 4 one of, if not *the*, safest high-performance cars available to the public.

1990

Further paring down, and consolidation, of the Porsche line for 1990 eliminates the 3.3–liter, 282 hp 911 Turbo from the U.S. market, and the 3.2–liter, 214 hp Carrera (in all three body styles) is replaced by the 3.6–liter, 247 hp Carrera 2 (the last time the Carrera 2 designation was used was on the two-liter, four-cam, four-cylinder Carrera in the early 1960s).

The Carrera 2 shares body and chassis (except the "2" has only rear drive while the "4" has four-wheel drive), with the Carrera 4 introduced in 1989. Both cars are available in Coupe, Targa, and Cabriolet body styles, and the Speedster was dropped after its brief (800 cars) 1989 production run.

One feature unique to the Carrera 2 is the Porsche Double Function (PDF) transmission, with driver's choice of fully automatic or full manual control.

Anti-lock brakes and drive and passenger side airbags are standard on all 1990 Porsches, and the Carrera 2 and 4 have force-sensitive power steering.

When the water-cooled, front-engined Porsches came along (924, 928 and 944) it seemed that the air-cooled, rear-engined

By careful attention to top detailing, including padding and insulation, the 911 Cabriolet is one of the quietest convertibles—except for the intrusion of the air-cooled rear engine noises. Well, at least wind noises are low. *Porsche*

911 series was at the end of its design rope, but it continues with no end in sight now. The 911 series are Porsches for customers who really like to drive, and take pride in their ability to drive. Any other Porsche model would be easier to drive at its maximum, but none can offer the sheer joy of flat-out motoring that can be realized from mastering the intricacies of a high-performance tail-heavy car.

In spite of who you may see driving a 911, it isn't a car for the dilettante driver, or one who wants maximum comfort and silence

A good comparison of the three 911 body types is shown here—Coupe, Targa and Cabriolet. All three models are the same mechanically, and in most other respects except for the top itself. *Porsche*

with an automatic transmission. It is a car for those who relish *getting* there as much as *being* there (sailors, as opposed to power boat drivers, feel the same way). The 911 series isn't easy to drive at maximum, but will highly reward those who can do it.

The slant-nose "935 look," called the 930S, became an option in 1987 for the 911 Turbo—for $23,244 extra. The sloping nose included retract-

able headlights, functional air vents behind the lights, and air scoops in front of the rear wheels for additional engine and brake cooling. *Porsche*

911SC, 930 Turbo (1978-) changes

Engine
Design: .... Air-cooled, flat (opposed) six
Borexstroke, mm/inches: 911SC 95x70.4/3.74x2.77
930 Turbo 97x74.4/3.82x2.93
Displacement, cc/cubic inches: 911SC 2993/182.57
930 Turbo 3299/201.24
Valve operation: Chain-driven single overhead camshaft on each bank with rocker arms & inclined valves
Compression ratio: 911SC .... 8.5:1, 9.8 (from 1981)
930 Turbo 7:1
Carburetion: 911SC .... Bosch K-Jetronic fuel injection
930 Turbo .... KKK Turbocharger & Bosch K-Jetronic fuel injection
BHP (Mfr): 911SC .... 180 DIN/172 SAE @5500, 204 DIN/196 SAE @5500 (from 1981)
Chassis & drivetrain
Transmission: 911SC .... Porsche five-speed, all-synchromesh
930 Turbo .... Porsche four-speed, all-synchromesh
Axle ratio: 911SC 3.875:1
930 Turbo 4.22:1
General
Wheelbase, mm/inches: 2271/89.4
Track, front, mm/inches: 911SC 1369/53.9
930 Turbo 1433/56.4
rear, mm/inches: 911SC 1379/54.3
930 Turbo 1501/59.1
Tire size, front & rear: 911SC .... 185/70 VR 15 & 215/60 VR 15
930 Turbo .... 205/55 VR 16 & 225/50 VR 16
Wheels, front & rear: 911SC .... Cast alloy 6J 15 & 7J 15
930 Turbo .... Forged alloy 7J 16 & 8J 16
Body builder: .... Porsche

911, Turbo (1985-89)

Engine
Design: .... Air-cooled flat (opposed) six
Borexstroke, mm/inches: 97.0x74.4/3.82x2.93
Displacement, cc/cubic inches: 3299/201
Valve operation: .... Chain-driven single overhead camshaft on each bank with rocker arms & inclined valves
Compression ratio: 7.0:1
Carburetion: .... Bosch K-Jetronic fuel injection
BHP (Mfr): .... 282 @ 5500
Chassis & drivetrain
Frame: .... Unit body
Component layout: .... Rear engine, rear drive
Clutch: .... Fichtel & Sachs single dry-plate
Transmission: .... Porsche four-speed
Axle ratio: 4.22:1
Transmission ratios: 2.25, 1.30, 0.89, 0.63:1
Rear suspension: ..... Independent, semi-trailing link on each side wiith transverse torsion bars & telescopic shock absorbers, anti-roll bar
Front suspension: .... Independent, MacPherson telescopic shock strut and triangulated wishbone on each side with longitudinal torsion bars, anti-roll bar
General
Wheelbase, mm/inches: 2271/89.4
Track, front, mm/inches: 1369/53.9
rear, mm/inches: 1379/54.3
Brakes: ..... Hydraulic, dual-circuit system, 4 ventilated discs, brake servo
Tire size, front & rear: 205/55 VR-16-245/45VR-16
Wheels, front & rear: .... J7-16/J9-16, cast aluminum
Body builder: .... Porsche

QUICK GUIDE TO THE 911 SERIES

Year	Model	Transmissions	Disp.	Wheelbs
1963	901	5-sp	1991cc	2211 mm
1964	911 (from Sept.)	5-sp	1991	2211
1965	911	4- or 5-sp	1991	2211
1966	911	4- or 5-sp	1991	2211
1967	911, 911S	Sporto, 4- or 5-sp	1991	2211
1968	911, 911L (U.S.), T, L, S (Eur)	Sporto, 4- or 5-sp	1991	2211
1969	911T, 911E, 911S	Sport (all but S), 4- or 5-sp	1991	2268
1970	911T, 911E, 911S	Sporto, 4- or 5-sp	2195	2268
1971	911T, 911E, 911S	Sporto, 4- or 5-sp	2195	2268
1972	911T, 911E, 911S	Sporto, 4- or 5-sp	2341	2271
1973	911T, 911E, 911S	Sporto, 4- or 5-sp	2341	2271
	Carrera 2.7 (track only, U.S.)	5-sp	2687	2271
1974	911, 911S, Carrera	Sporto, 4- or 5-sp	2687	2271
	Carrera RS, RSR	5-sp	2993	2271
1975	911S Carrera	Sporto, 4- or 5-sp	2687	2271
	Carrera RS, RSR, Turbo	4-sp	2993	2271
1976	911S	Sporto, 4- or 5-sp	2687	2271
	Carrera 3.0 (Eur) Turbo Carrera 930 (U.S.)	4-sp	2993	2271
1977	911, 911S	Sporto, 4- or 5-sp	2687	2271
	Carrera 3.0 (Eur) Turbo Carrera 930 (U.S.)	4-sp	2993	2271
1978	911SC	Sporto, 4- or 5-sp	2993	2271
	Turbo	4-sp	3299	2271
1979	911SC	5-sp	2993	2271
	Turbo	4-sp	3299	2271
1980	911SC	5-sp	2993	2271
	Turbo (Europe only)	4-sp	3299	2271
1981	911SC	5-sp	2993	2271
	Turbo (Europe only)	4-sp	3299	2271
1982	911SC	5-sp	2993	2271
	Turbo (Europe only)	4-sp	3299	2271
1983	911SC	5-sp	2993	2771
	Turbo (Europe only)	4-sp	3299	2271
1984	911 Carrera	5-sp	3164	2271
	Turbo (Europe only)	4-sp	3299	2271
1985	911 Carrera	5-sp	3164	2271
	Turbo (Europe only)	4-sp	3299	2271
1986	911 Carrera	5-sp	3164	2271
	Turbo (U.S. and Europe)	4-sp	3299	2271
1987	911 Carrera	5-sp	3164	2271
	Turbo (U.S. and Europe)	4-sp	3299	2271
1988	911 Carrera	5-sp	3164	2271
	911 Turbo	4-sp	3299	2271
1989	911 Carrera	5-sp	3164	2271
	911 Turbo	5-sp	3299	2271
	911 Carrera 4	5-sp	3601	2271
1990	911 Carrera 2	5-sp	3601	2271
	911 Carrera 4	5-sp	3601	2271

63-69 2.0
70-71 2.2
72-73 2.4
74-77 2.7
78-83 3.0
84-89 3.2
90- 3.6

911 Turbo
75-77 3.0
78-79 3.3
86-93 3.3

Unfortunately, the third, high-mounted, taillight now required in the U.S. poses a problem that designers can't always solve—particularly in a retrofit situation. The light for the Coupe can be concealed in the rear window, but it won't work for the Targa and Cabriolet, so the light sticks out of the body above the engine grille. *Porsche*

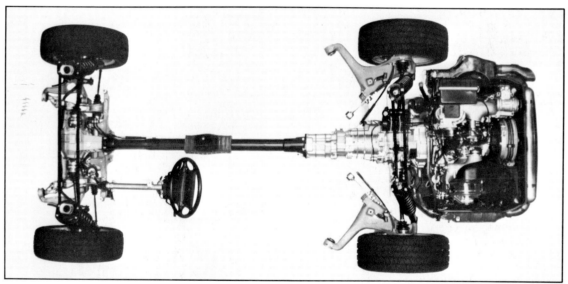

The ultimate in chassis sophistication: four-wheel drive with computer-managed traction distribution via multiple-disc clutches in center and rear differentials, and ABS make the Carrera 4 the supreme high-performance machine. *Porsche*

The Carrera 4 spoiler lifts automatically at about 40 mph, and retracts flush with the body at about 6 mph; all in the interest of downforce

when needed for maximum traction and anti-lift. *Porsche*

For 1990, the Carrera 2 was added. Based on the chassis of the Carrera 4, it also has coil-spring suspension, anti-lock brakes, a speed actuated rear spoiler (which raises at 40 mph and retracts flush with the rear body at 6 mph). Like other 911 models, the Carrera 2 has only rear-wheel drive. *Porsche*

A feature unique (so far) to the Carrera 2 is the "Tiptronic" shift; a system that allows full automatic transmission shifting when the lever is in the left slot. When the lever is in the right side of the gate shifting is fully manual—with a push forward to upshift, a pull back to downshift, but with no clutch pedal to push. *Porsche*

The Carrera 4, introduced in 1989, was the first of the 911 series to have a completely new chassis/floor pan, and had coil springs instead of torsion bars. Utilizing technology gained from development of the 959, the "4" was the most sophisticated and complex Porsche ever made available to the general public as a production model. It has full-time four-wheel drive and anti-lock brakes. *Porsche*

Carrera 2 & 4

Engine
Design: .... Air-cooled flat (opposed) six
Borexstroke, mm/inches: .... 100.0 x 76.4/3.94 x 3.01
Displacement, cc/cubic inches: 3601/220
Valve operation: .... Chain-driven single overhead camshaft on each bank, two inclined valves per cylinder
Compression ratio: 11.3:1
Carburetion: .... Bosch Motronic with port fuel injection
BHP (Mfr): .... 247 SAE @ 6100

Chassis & drivetrain
Frame: .... Steel, unit body
Component layout: Carrera 2 .... Rear engine, rear-wheel drive
Carrera 4 .... Rear engine, four-wheel drive
Clutch: .... Single dry plate

Transmission: .... Porsche five-speed, all-synchromesh
Axle ratio: .... (limited-slip) 3.44:1
Rear suspension: .... Independent, semi-trailing arms, coil springs, anti-roll bar
Front suspension: ...... Independent, struts and lower control arms, coil springs, anti-roll bar

General
Wheelbase, mm/inches: 2271/89.4
Track, front, mm/inches: 1380/54.3
rear, mm/inches: 1374/54.1
Brakes: .... Ventilated disc, ABS
Tire size, front: .... Goodyear Eagle ZR 205/55ZR-16
rear: .... Goodyear Eagle ZR 225/50ZR-16
Wheels: .... Forged aluminum
Body builder: .... Porsche

★★

Chapter 8

912

When the Porsche 911 was introduced for sale in the fall of 1964 as a 1965 model, it was met with enthusiastic response from all quarters, but its high price eliminated many potential buyers. Porsche management felt that this was not in the best interests of the company. It appeared that Porsche could sell all the 911s it could produce, but the market "base" was too narrow for Porsche's goals.

In 1965, the lowest-priced 911 was the equivalent of $5,496 in West Germany, which was an increase of about $1,500 more than the 356 1600SC. While the 911 price wasn't out of line, considering quality, handling and performance, it was quite a bit more than old Porsche customers (other than the few who had bought Carreras) were used to paying.

Typically, Porsche management had considered this possibility so the problem was solved quickly and directly for the home market in April 1965: Install the old four-cylinder pushrod Porsche engine in the new body to create a lower-priced Porsche. Americans didn't get the new car, the 912, however, until September 1965 when 356 production came to an end.

The 912 engine was the familiar 1582 cc flat-four, with pushrods and rocker arms, as used in the 356 series, and it was taken more directly from the SC—slightly detuned from 95 to 90 hp. Because of the 911/912 body's slightly better aerodynamics, ninety horsepower was sufficient to propel the 2,190-pound 912 to 115 miles per hour, which was

marginally better than the 356SC, even with its five more horsepower.

The 912 weighed 220 pounds less than the comparable 911, and weight distribution improved from 41/59 of the 911 to 44/56 for the 912.

A 12-volt electrical system was standard on both the 911 and 912, which was a vast improvement over the six volts of the 356 series. Both four- and five-speed transmissions were available. The five-speed, which had second, third, fourth and fifth in the usual H-pattern, with first and reverse to the left of the H, was basically the same gearbox as used in the 904, but turned around in the chassis.

If the lesser performance of the 912 was considered a disadvantage compared to the 911 (which had forty more horsepower), the lower price of the 912 was a resounding advantage.

A *Car and Driver* report in the October 1965 issue priced a five-speed 912 at $4,696, while a month earlier *The Autocar* (London) listed a 912 at £2,040 plus £426 purchase tax, or £2,466 (about $6,500 at the then-current $2.80-per-British-Pound exchange rate). The 911, at that time, was selling for about $6,300 in the United States. As usual, American buyers fared better than their English counterparts.

Some Porsche enthusiasts, and magazine road testers, complained about the Spartan interior of the 912, but this was only obvious if you had just stepped out of a 911. The three dials on the panel of the 912—speed-ometer, tach and combined fuel and temperature gauges—were similar to the panel of the 356C models which the 912 replaced, so things were relatively comparable.

The 912 was mainly austere in its performance (again, mainly if compared to the 911) and, to some extent, visually. It had many of the comfort, and all of the safety, features of the 911, including three-speed wipers, windshield washer, rear window defroster, back-up light and reclining seats. During the 1965 model run, both the 911 and 912 were available with the Webasto gasoline heater and, in September, the Targa body style.

Improvements to the 912 came steadily, as they did (and do) on other Porsche models,

and in 1966 the track was widened. In 1967 the five-dial dash became standard in the 912, and safety door locks were added. Interior carpeting was upgraded, and new engine mounts were fitted.

Generally speaking, all running changes made to the 911 (with the exception of the engine) were made to the 912 at the same time. This was a production economy, but one that was beneficial to the buyer at the same time. When the 1969 models were introduced, the wheelbase had been lengthened on both the 911 and 912 by installing longer rear trailing links. These 2¼ inches of extra wheelbase improved weight distribution by a small amount, but improved handling even more. The engines in both cars remained in the same location, but the

The 912 (this is a 1969) was so much like the 911 in appearance that only very knowledgeable observers could spot the difference without looking inside to see the less-fancy interior or into the engine compartment. The rear lid had "912" just below the air intake grille. *Porsche+ Audi*

The 912, introduced in April 1965, didn't go to the American market until September 1965 when the 356C went out of production. The 912 was almost indistinguishable from the 911 in general appearance, but had "912" on its rear lid, and a plainer interior with only three instruments in the dash compared to the five of the 911. *Porsche+Audi*

half-shafts were canted backward in plan view from the transmission toward the outer hubs.

The least expensive 912 cost more than $5,000 by 1969, and could top $6,000 if all the available options were ordered. This seems like a tremendous bargain today; and it was a bargain then, considering the buyer got the same quality and most of the handling and performance that the owner of a 911 received. But there were problems related to the reduced horsepower in a car that looked faster than it was, and had a reputation for performance that many 912 drivers seemed to feel obligated to maintain.

The 911 driver could indulge in the "stoplight grand prix" and, if he showed reasonable restraint, wouldn't harm the car's rugged six-cylinder power plant. The 911 was as fast as it looked, and could give a good account of itself on road, track or drag strip.

The 912 driver, on the other hand, had to push his car harder, and even then couldn't begin to achieve the performance of the 911. And, if he tried it often enough, the engine suffered abuse that drastically shortened its life.

Also, too many mechanics, and some owners, thought the 912 engine was "just another Volkswagen" and this muddled thinking could prove fatal to the 912 engine. It was a Porsche design through and through, and needed good care and maintenance by a qualified Porsche mechanic or a knowledgeable owner.

By the end of 1969, the 912 was phased out to make way for the 914 and 914/6, which were to fill the price gap below the 911.

Americans missed the 912 more than did the Europeans, probably because of different driving habits. Driving styles, partly due to heritage, and partly from government and state speed restrictions, differed between Europe/England and the United States. The American buyer accepted the 912 for what it was intended to be and very likely was not as hard on his car as the European, who was used to flat-out driving most of the time.

About the time the 924 was being introduced in Europe as the new low-priced

Instrument panel of the 912 is one of the major differences that sets it apart visually from the 911. Bodies and suspension are enough alike that only the experts can tell the difference. *Porsche Werkfoto*

Porsche, the 912 was reintroduced in the United States as the "E" model. This time, however, the engine really was a Volkswagen unit—from the VW 411 via the Porsche 914 two-liter.

It was in the fall of 1975 that the 912E (for *Einspritzung*, or injection) came out as the 1976 model. The chassis/body shared all the improvements that had been made to the 911 since the last 912 in 1969, and the engine shared the modifications received by the last 914.

The 94x71 mm bore and stroke resulted in 1971 cc displacement. With 7.6:1 compression ratio and Bosch fuel injection, it still had 90 DIN horsepower, as did the previous 912, but SAE power was now rated at 86 net, all at 4900 rpm. A five-speed transmission was standard for the 1976 912 which made the car seem more sporting, but performance suffered because the weight had gone up 400 pounds in six years. Acceleration was down because of the weight increase, and top speed was down because of more aerodynamic drag from fender flares, U.S. bumpers, and so forth.

The buyer of a used 912 will get most of the same attributes that the buyer of a used 911 will get: the same general appearance, the same quality, almost the same handling, equal comfort, accommodation and cargo capacity, and a car which he will be proud to own and drive. If it's a 1976, he'll also get the galvanized body antirust prevention of the 911. His steering and brakes will be as good, which will make the driver's confidence in the safety as good as he could get with the 911.

What the 912 driver won't get is the sparkling performance from the extra horsepower that's available in the 911 and its derivatives. It would seem that all this won't cost the 912 owner as much, and that's correct—to a point. Initial cost should be far less than a 911, just as it was when these comparable cars were new, but maintenance cost will not be in the same ratio as purchase price. Chassis maintenance for the two should be comparable. Engine maintenance for the 912 will be somewhat less than that for the 911, but not as much less as you might expect.

A few mechanics will recommend replacing the 912 engine with a six if major repair work is needed, but I don't subscribe to that philosophy. The 1965–69 912 crankshaft (which is from the 356SC) is the weak link in the engine and, whereas a new 912 crankshaft will cost in the neighborhood of $3,735 (late 1989), a 356C crank can be purchased for around $1,280. A rebuild with a C crank should end most of a 912's engine problems, but will lower the rev limit from 6000 to 5500. A good, non-factory German forged crank, from the original dies is now available for about $1,800 (1989 prices). Also, a lower-quality Brazilian-made copy can be bought, but I don't recommend it.

In either a 911 or 912, the worst rust, if any, will be found at the bottom of the front fenders just ahead of the doors, at the top of the rear fenders just behind the door, and around the turn signal/taillight housings. Check the front trunk carefully, especially around the battery (or batteries) and at the front mount for the A-arms. Poke around the rear torsion bar tube—rust repair here can be very costly.

If you're looking for Porsche design, Porsche quality, Porsche handling, Porsche safety and Porsche looks, and don't need blazing performance, the 912 may be just the ticket. The 912 has, or will accept, all Porsche equipment and accessories that the 911 will accommodate, but won't have the acceleration and top speed. It takes a very special car owner to be content for long with a car of this type when it's underpowered compared to its look-alike brethren. It's your choice.

---

912 Coupe, Targa (1965-69), 912E (1976)

Engine
Design: .... Air-cooled flat (opposed) four
Borexstroke, mm/inches: 1965–69 .... 82.5x74/3.25x2.91
1976 .... 94x71/3.70x2.80
Displacement, cc/cubic inches: 1965–69 .... 1582/96.5
1976 .... 1971/120.2
Valve operation: .... Single camshaft with pushrods & rocker arms
Compression ratio: 1965–69 .... 9.3:1
1976 .... 7.6:1
Carburetion: 1965–69 .... Two Solex 40 PII-4
1976 .... Bosch fuel injection
BHP (Mfr): 1965–69 .... 90 DIN/102 SAE @ 5800
1976 .... 90 DIN/86 SAE @ 4900

Chassis & drivetrain
Frame: .... Unit body
Component layout: .... Rear engine, rear drive
Clutch: .... Fichtel & Sachs single dry-plate
Transmission: 1965 ...... Porsche four-speed, all-synchromesh
1966–69 ...... Porsche four- or five-speed, all-synchromesh
1976 .... Porsche five-speed, all-synchromesh

Axle ratio: 4.43:1
Rear suspension: ...... Independent, semi-trailing link on each side with transverse torsion bars & telescopic shock absorbers
Front suspension: .... Independent, MacPherson telescopic shock strut and triangulated wishbone on each side with longitudinal torsion bars & anti-roll bar

General
Wheelbase, mm/inches: 1965–68 .... 2211/87.1
1969 .... 2268/89.3
1976 .... 2272/89.4
Track, front, mm/inches: 1965 .... 1337/52.6
1966–68 .... 1351/53.2
1969 & 1976 .... 1361/53.6
rear, mm/inches: 1965 .... 1317/51.9
1966–68 .... 1321/52.0
1969 & 1976 .... 1346/53.0
Brakes: .... Ate-Dunlop disc
Tire size, front & rear: 1965–69 .... 165-15 SP
1976 .... 165-15 HR
Wheels: 1965–69 .... Bolt-on, steel disc
1976 .... Pressure-cast alloy
Body builder .... Porsche

The 912 was revived in 1976 after the 914 was dropped, and looked even more like the 911. The new 912E had the four-cylinder, fuel-injected engine from the VW 411 and was rated at 32 highway mpg by the EPA. *Porsche+Audi*

Chapter 9

| ★★ | 914/4 |
| ★★★ | 914/6 |

914/4 and 914/6

In Karl Ludvigsen's book, *Porsche: Excellence Was Expected*, the philosophy, development and production of the 914, 914/6 and 916 occupy fifty-two pages. It is a fascinating exercise worked out with the cooperation of three of Germany's automotive industrial giants: Porsche, Volkswagen and Karmann. For our purposes, the explanation can be more brief. I recommend Ludvigsen's book to anyone who wants to go into more depth than is possible here.

Dr. Ferdinand Porsche had designed the Auto Union racing cars in 1933 to carry their engines in what was then called the "rear" and is now called "mid" position. When he designed the Volkswagen, and later the Porsche road cars, he put the lightweight air-cooled engine behind the rear axle in what was truly the "rear" location. However, when Porsche resumed competition in 1953, those cars carried their engines behind the driver but ahead of the rear axle once more.

Porsche management believed that the trend of the future might well be toward the mid-engined road car, and it could have been their own racing successes that gave them the impetus to proceed. Porsche's all-out racing machines had all been designed with the engine in front of the rear axle: 550 Spyder, 550A/1500RS, RSK, RS 60 and 61, Formula 1 and 2, 904 GTS, 906, 908 and 917.

Mid-engine-placement advantages for a racing car are too numerous to repeat them all, but the major ones are: compactness,

with resulting light weight which aids acceleration and reduces braking effort; low polar moment of inertia (from a central grouping of major heavy components) which makes the responsiveness better, although it takes a better driver to recover from an incipient spin in this type of car; and good weight distribution.

The disadvantages, which would have to be overcome for a customer road car (luggage space, sound deadening for the engine location is just behind the passenger compartment, and chassis construction which would allow easy access to both passenger and engine compartments) are simply ignored for the racing cars.

Porsche management's desire to produce a relatively inexpensive car came coincidentally with Volkswagen's (under the direction of Heinz Nordhoff) plan to produce a sportier car to help broaden the VW image away from a producer of strictly utilitarian transportation. It also came at a time when Volkswagen wanted to drop the Type 2 Karmann-Ghia, which was not selling well.

After meetings between Ferry Porsche and Heinz Nordhoff, an agreement was reached whereby Porsche would design a new car for Volkswagen (to use the new 411 engine) which would be called a VW-Porsche. But Porsche retained the right to buy back body shells in which Porsche could install its own engine.

The new project would be a two-way benefit to Volkswagen because the 914, as it

The 914/4, 1972 model shown, was an agile and responsive car due to its mid-engine placement and resultant low polar moment of inertia.

Engine access and luggage space suffered, although there were luggage compartments in front and at the rear. *Porsche+Audi*

The 914/6 could be identified by five-lug wheels. Shown here are Mahle die-cast magnesium wheels which were optional. *Porsche+Audi*

was to be called, would replace the 1500 Karmann-Ghia and, at the same time, the new car would be assembled at Karmann's factory in Osnabruck. Thus, VW would get its sportier car, Karmann would use it to replace the production of the Ghia, and at the same time keep its trained workforce employed, and Porsche would be able to get bodies directly from Karmann to use as it saw fit.

The body shape was based on a design by Gugelot GmbH which was originally intended to be a front-engined car made from layers of fiberglass bonded together with a foam layer inside the "sandwich." BMW, Daimler-Benz, Volkswagen, Karmann and Porsche were all interested, and conducted tests of the materials. The conclusion was that it wouldn't work for mass production.

A Porsche team, directed by Butzi Porsche, changed the Gugelot design to accommodate the mid-engine placement, and made other styling changes to suit Porsche's needs or desires. Before the 914 got into production, however, Nordhoff died in April 1968, and the new director of Volkswagen, Kurt Lotz, denied Porsche some of the agreement terms that had been verbal between Porsche and Nordhoff.

As a result, Porsche and Volkswagen entered into a joint marketing venture, creating the VG (Vertriebsgesellschaft), whereby each company owned exactly fifty percent of the sales organization which would now handle Volkswagen, Porsche and Audi; and Porsche could buy bodies from Karmann, but at a much higher price than Porsche had expected.

The final outcome of all this negotiation and agreement, was that Karmann built the 914 as an out-the-door-ready-to-go car bearing the VW-Porsche name for Europe, and just Porsche for America. The 914/6 bodies were assembled, trimmed and painted in Karmann's Osnabruck facility but were shipped to Porsche for final assembly where they went down the same production line with the 911.

Public introduction of the 914 was at the Frankfurt auto show in September 1969, and the first cars reached German showrooms in February 1970, with the American versions arriving in U.S. showrooms in March 1970.

Porsche's first advertising for the 914 played up the benefits of the mid-engine car's handling by saying, "If there's one thing we've learned from racing, it's where to put the engine . . . We think it's time you shared those advantages. So we've built a couple of mid-engined cars for the street." After listing several reasons why this configuration is better, including low center of gravity, handling, braking, tire life and safety, Porsche concluded with: "So if you're thinking about a true, two-seat sports car, think about this: When you don't get a back seat, you should at least get an engine in its place."

At the Frankfurt show introduction in 1969, the 914 was priced at DM 11,955, and the 914/6 at DM 18,992 which, when translated into U.S. dollars, worked out to $3,015 and $4,775. By the time the cars arrived in the United States in March, advertisements gave the prices (East Coast) at $3,495 and 914/6 at $5,595 (with a note at the bottom of the page: "Prices subject to change without notice."). A $200 Appearance Group was available for the 914, which included chrome bumpers and chrome-trimmed vinyl covering for the roof pillars. Car prices were $100 higher on the West Coast.

While the appearance of the 914 was a departure for Porsche, the mechanical pieces were familiar. The MacPherson telescopic shock strut front suspension with its longitudinal torsion bars was taken almost intact from the 911; but while the rear trailing link independent suspension had similar geometry to the 911, the links themselves and the coil springs were new.

Both 914s had disc brakes at all four wheels with solid rotors at the back. The 914/4 also had solid rotors at the front, but the 914/6 had vented rotors. Both cars had dual master cylinders which activated the separate front/rear brake systems with a rear brake pressure limiter. The hand brake on the 914/4 was of the caliper type, but the 914/6 utilized the drum-type hand brake of the 911. The 914's 4.5–15 wheels mounted to VW 411 four-lug hubs, while the 914/6 came with 5.5–14 or 5.5–15 (optional) alloy

Standard 914 for U.S. had side-marker lights just behind front turn indicator lights, and this early European version had driving lights set into bumper face-bar. Later U.S. versions had optional driving/fog lights. *Porsche+Audi*

The 914 interior harks back to the 356 Speedster for austere simplicity. *Porsche+Audi*

European 914s carried the Wolfsburg crest in the steering wheel center because the car was sold in Volkswagen showrooms, while the U.S. 914 carried the Porsche crest in its steering wheel because of the Porsche+Audi distributorship, and was sold through Porsche dealers. *Porsche+Audi*

or 5.5–15 steel wheels attached to Porsche five-lug hubs. Wheels were stamped steel for the base 914 but the 914/6 had ten-spoke Mahle alloy wheels; or more commonly 5½x14 forged Fuchs five-spoke alloy wheels.

Boge shocks were standard with gas-pressure Bilsteins available as an option, and neither 914/4 nor 914/6 had anti-roll bars standard, as Porsche engineers thought they weren't needed. With the factory-recommended tire pressures, 26 psi front and 29 rear, to compensate for the 46/54 front/rear weight bias, both the four and six had near-neutral handling. Engineer Helmuth Bott said the 914 was about six-to-eight-percent better (cornering) than a comparable 911. If the 914 was driven into a corner at below maximum speed it had just a bit of understeer, but if pushed hard into a corner it would display oversteer.

Power for the 914 came from the new Volkswagen 411, and was the "traditional" four-cylinder flat (opposed), air-cooled overhead-valve design. In this application the Bosch fuel-injected 1967 cc unit produced 80 DIN horsepower with a net SAE rating of 76. The fuel injection, developed by Bosch under Bendix patents, allowed the early 914 and VW 411 to meet the U.S. emission standards without using an air pump. The 1975 and 1976 914s had air pumps.

The 914/6 shared the six-cylinder, single overhead cam engine with the 1968–69 911T (the 1970–71 911T had a 2.2-liter engine). This engine had capacitive discharge ignition system, dry-sump lubrication system as on the 911—the oil reservoir tank was on the left side of the engine compartment—and two triple-choke Weber carburetors. In this form it produced 110 DIN and 105 SAE net horsepower. The six-cylinder engine ran usually ten degrees hotter than the four, which was notorious for overheating. One 914 owner says that some oil-temperature gauges were inconsistent, and because the 914/4 gauge was not marked with actual numbers, it was difficult to know what the temperature really was. He calibrated his, after getting tired of driving slowly because it got into the red so often, and found the *start* of the red section was 195 degrees.

The fuel pump on the 914/4 was located immediately adjacent to the right heat exchanger, causing vapor lock. Oil temperature gauges were unmarked, but the cars got hot when driven for long distances at high speeds. Like all other air-cooled Porsches, 914s are subject to starter solenoid/electrical system overheating. When driven long distances in high temperatures, the cars wouldn't restart. The culprit is unclear: starter, solenoid, bad ground, ignition switch, etc. Vapor lock was the car's worst problem. The demise of the car could partly have been Porsche's lack of a cure for vapor lock from 1970 to 1975, when the fuel pump was relocated to a cooler position up front.

There were no transmission options (the Sportomatic had been "advertised" as an available option for both cars, but I can find no evidence that this unit ever appeared in a production 914 or 914/6) and both cars used the five-speed assembly from the 911. Because of the engine location, the transmission was turned around and the ring gear installed on the opposite side of the pinion gear. The axle ratio was 4.428:1 on both cars.

The unitized steel body was strictly for two passengers, and had no provision for additional seating. It did have more luggage space than would be expected from a car of this size, or from a mid-engined car, by having two luggage compartments. One was behind the engine, over the transmission; the other was at the front, with the spare tire.

In addition to the bigger, more powerful engine, the 914/6 was fancier and better equipped. It had three-speed windshield wipers, electric windshield washers and chrome-plated bumpers. The 914 had painted bumpers, and the driver had to activate the pneumatic windshield washers by hand. The six also had headlight flasher, hand throttle, dual-tone horns, external trim strips, wider ten-spoke wheels and vinyl trim on the "roll bar."

The instrument panel contained three dials, the center one being a tachometer which went to 7000 on the 914 and 8000 on the 914/6. At the right was a speedometer (120 mph for the four and 150 for the six). The left dial on each model carried a fuel-level indicator at the bottom, but the top of the dial on the bigger-engined model displayed oil temperature, while the top part of the 914's left dial had warning lights for fuel level, hand brake and low brake fluid.

The one-piece fiberglass roof (only the part between the windshield and the Targa-type roll bar) was easily removed and stowed in the rear luggage compartment.

No right-hand-drive models were made for those countries that drive on the left side of the road but conversions were made by Crayford Auto Developments, Ltd., in Kent, England.

During the six years of production for the 914—1970 into the 1976 model year—and three years for the 914/6 which ended in 1972, the cars remained basically the same. Porsche has always made running changes except in major components, so minor details were improved over the model run. This led indirectly to the demise of the 914. It was never as well developed as other Porsches.

For the 1972 models, introduced at the Frankfurt show in September 1971, the passenger's seat was made adjustable—fore and aft movement as well as tilt being the same as in the 914/6. Windshield wiper and washer controls were mounted on the steering column, as on the 914/6, instead of on the panel, and the glovebox doorknob was enlarged. Adjustable air outlets were mounted at each end of the dash. Insulation and sound deadening were improved. Wider wheels, part of the Appearance Group for America, were added to the European option list. For 1973, the driver's seat was adjustable and the shift linkage improved. These improvements were significant enough to make it wise to buy a 1973–or–later 914/4.

The EA-series four-cylinder engine, which would run on regular fuel, replaced the W-series engine of the original 914, but changes to the fuel-injection system mandated no performance loss.

A 2.0–liter engine was optional from 1973 on, but in 1974 the 914's standard engine displacement was increased to 1795 cc (109.5 cubic inches) by increasing the bore from 90 to 93 mm, and displacement was increased again in 1975 by enlarging the bore to 94 mm, and lengthening the stroke from 66 to 71 mm with a resulting displacement of 1971 cc, or 120.3 CID. These latter 914s can be spotted by the 2.0 numbers on the rear lid. The 914/6 remained at 1991 cc (121.5 CID) during its nearly three-year tenure. Built primarily as 1970 and 1971 models, probably less than fifty sixes were built for the 1972 model year.

No 914 ever carried the Porsche crest on the hood as it came from the factory, and if you find one today you can bet it was installed by some owner along the way somewhere. The Porsche name was carried on the rear deck inlet, and the Porsche crest was in the center of the steering wheel on U.S. models while the VW crest was carried on the steering wheel of European models. Hubcaps on the European 914 came straight from the VW 411, and the U.S. 914/4 had the same caps but without the VW logo. The 914/6 had a Porsche crest on the hubcaps if it was equipped with steel wheels.

The reason for not openly identifying the 914 series as Porsches stems not from company indifference, or lack of pride in the cars, but rather from a marketing decision by Porsche and VW management.

The 914 was to be sold in America as a Porsche, but in the rest of the world it would be a VW-Porsche. Management of the newly-created Porsche+Audi (which in America was a division of VW of America) marketing decreed that dealers would have to set up separate facilities, away from the VW showrooms, for their Porsche and Audi cars. The dealer could sell all three cars, but not on the same premises. Because Porsche+Audi wanted to separate VW from Porsche in the minds of the buyers, the 914 didn't carry the

By utilizing both front and rear compartments, quite a bit of luggage could be carried—assuming careful planning and packing. The 1973 had big rubber bumper guards at the front, the '74 had them front and back, and '75 and '76 had the "crash bumpers" shown above. *Porsche+ Audi*

The 914/6 engine was from the 911T, but mounted ahead of the rear axle in the 914. *Porsche+ Audi*

VW-Porsche name as it did elsewhere.

The reception of the 914 was not overwhelming and, in some cases, was not even gracious. Appearance was the first stumbling block. Most viewers didn't like it at all, and most of the rest were lukewarm. Reports on the 914 damned it with faint praise. They liked the handling but hated the shift mechanism (although the side-shifter transaxle introduced in 1973 was a great improvement), and performance was not considered to be up to Porsche standards or

tradition. It was noisy by comparison to almost any other car, including Porsches. *Car and Driver* said it was half the cost of a 911, and half as good. And even without the VW name on the car, many still considered it more VW than Porsche, overlooking the fact that the first Porsches had almost all VW mechanical parts.

So what did the 914 offer? Besides reliability and economy it had competition potential. Its inherent balance and subsequent handling brought out the competitive spirit in many Porsche fans who hadn't thought in those terms in recent years. We eventually saw 914s in races, rallies, auto crosses and slaloms on both club and national levels. Many were raced in international events with success.

But more than that, it was and is the affordable Porsche, at least in 914 form. The 914/6 is now considered one of the sought-after Porsches and prices are getting higher at a rapid rate. Converting a 914 to "six" status isn't advisable, for any number of reasons, not the least important of which is

914 & 914/6 (1970–75)

Engine
Design: 914 . . . . Air-cooled flat (opposed) four
914/6 . . . . Air-cooled flat (opposed) six
Borexstroke, mm/inches: 1970–73 four 90x66/3.54x2.60
1974–76 four 93x66/3.66x2.60
1973–1976 four 94x71/3.70x2.80
all 914/6 . . . . 80x66/3.15x2.60
Displacement, cc/cubic inches: 1970–73 four 1679/102.3
1974–76 four 1795/109.5
1973–1976 four 1971/120.3
all 914/6 . . . . 1991/121.5
Valve operation: 914 . . . . Single camshaft with pushrods & rocker arms; inclined exhaust valves
914/6 . . . . . . Chain-driven single overhead camshaft on each bank with rocker arms & inclined valves
Compression ratio: 1.7-liter four 8.2:1
1.8-liter four 7.3:1
2.0-liter four 7.6:1
914/6 . . . . 8.6:1
Carburetion: all U.S. fours . . . . (European models had Solex carbs) Bosch fuel injection
914/6 . . . . Two Weber 40 IDT 3V carburetors
BHP (Mfr): 1.7-liter four . . . . 80 DIN/76 SAE @ 4900
1.8-liter four . . . . 76 DIN/72 SAE @ 4800
2.0-liter four . . . . 95 DIN/91 SAE @ 4900
914/6 . . . . 110 DIN/105 SAE @ 5800
Chassis & drivetrain
Frame: . . . . Unit body
Component layout: . . . . Mid-engine, rear drive
Clutch: . . . . Fichtel & Sachs single dry-plate
Transmission: . . . . Porsche five-speed, all-synchromesh
Axle ratio: 4.428:1
Rear suspension: . . . . . . Independent, semi-trailing link on each side, coil springs & telescopic shock absorbers
Front suspension: . . . . MacPherson telescopic shock strut and wishbone on each side with longitudinal torsion bars
General
Wheelbase, mm/inches: 2450/96.5
Track, front, mm/inches: (with 4½Jx15 wheels) 1331/52.4
(with 5½Jx15 wheels) 1343/52.9
rear, mm/inches: (with 4½Jx15 wheels) 1371/54.0
(with 5½Jx15 wheels) 1383/54.4
Brakes: . . . . Ate disc
Tire size, front & rear: . . . . . . 155 HR 15, 165 HR 15 or 185 HR 14 depending on wheels
Wheels: . . . . Bolt-on steel disc or pressure-cast alloy
Body builder: . . . . Karmann

All 914s had the removable roof section and fixed Targa-type roll-over bar. The only Porsche identifying feature on the outside was the lettering on the engine air intake behind the roll bar. This is a 1971 model. *Porsche+Audi*

The 1972 four-cylinder 914 carried only that number on the rear panel; the six would carry 914-6 in the same spot. *Porsche+Audi*

cost, and the fact that any Porsche enthusiast will recognize it as non-genuine. Serial numbers, which will tell the buyer what he's getting, are very easy to decipher.

More than 127,000 914s were made, but good, clean cars are not easy to find, so they hold their value well. Prices are now on the upswing.

The 914/4 engine is basically very stout, but the fuel injection system can give trouble. Even the newest 914 is fifteen years old, and the early electronic injection systems are not very reliable. Many cars have already been converted to carburetion, which is not difficult.

When you inspect a 914 for rust, check carefully under the battery tray in the engine compartment, around jack points, exhaust system, and inside rear seam of the rear trunk.

Be sure the right rear wheel alignment is correct. Acid from the battery can weaken the chassis in this area, causing the trailing arm to pull away from the chassis.

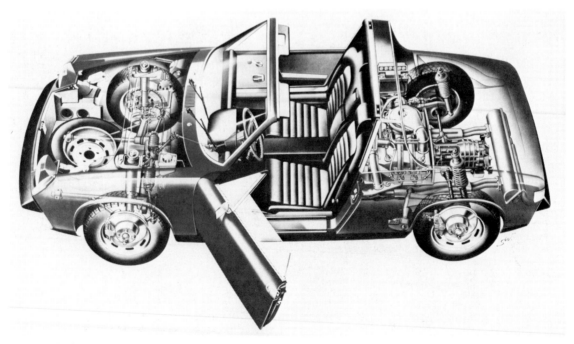

Phantom view of the 914/4 shows the basic mechanical layout of both four- and six-cylinder versions. *Porsche+Audi*

The U.S. version of the 914 received the European-style bumper-mounted driving lights in 1972. Also new were improved ventilation and an adjustable passenger seat as standard, but no other visual changes. *Porsche+Audi*

Introduced in April 1974 was a limited-edition 2.0-liter 914 which had a front spoiler, Mahle cast-alloy wheels, a special interior and only black or white body colors with contrasting yellow or orange, respectively, accent trim. *Porsche+ Audi*

For 1975, the 1914 received new energy-absorbing impact safety bumpers which had 2.5 inches of "give" via hydro-pneumatic dampers and new wheels; but the basic body remained as before. *Porsche+Audi*

Center console on the 914 was an option. It contained instruments instead of the usual warning lights. This car also has the optional factory air conditioning, which takes up a lot of space in the front trunk compartment. *Porsche+Audi*

Chapter 10

924 and
924 Turbo

The Porsche 924 was the most "different" Porsche the company had built in twenty-five years, yet it continued a philosophy of the first cars from this company—using Volkswagen parts as the basis for the vehicle.

The first 356 in 1950 had VW suspension, brakes, steering and a Porsche-modified VW air-cooled VW engine mounted at the back. The 924 had VW suspension, brakes, steering and a water-cooled VW engine mounted at the front. One major difference, aside from the air/water cooling, was that while the 356 used many VW components, it was designed to be a Porsche and sold as such. The 924, on the other hand, was designed by Porsche to be a VW—and ended up becoming a Porsche.

As far back as 1970, the VW-Porsche VG (Vertriebsgesellschaft—the joint organization formed to market the 914) saw that there was a probability that the 914 was not going to become the lasting favorite that the 356 had been. VG management therefore began planning a new car; one to be designed *by* Porsche *for* VG to sell as a VW/Audi—no more "VW-Porsche" in Europe and "Porsche" elsewhere, as the 914 had been conceived.

Requirements for the new car were formally outlined: 1. Interior space comparable to the 911; 2. Useful trunk volume; 3. Higher comfort level than the 914; 4. Maximum use of high-volume VW parts; 5. Technical similarity and family resemblance to 928 (this

car was in the design stage actually before the 924); 6. Not to be rear-engined or mid-engined; 7. Independent suspension all around; 8. 2+2 seating.

Once the parameters had been agreed to, the components that would form the basis for the new car were selected by a process of logical application as would be expected. It was understood that air-cooled engines were nearing the end of their production at both Porsche and Volkswagen so one of the new water-cooled units under development would be used. The one selected was a Volkswagen design, built by Audi, used in carbureted form in the VW LT van, the American Motors Pacer and Spirit, and in fuel-injected form in the new-to-be Porsche.

A mid-engine location was deemed unsatisfactory because of the 2+2 seating requirement, and a rear location á la 911 was ruled out because of the required family resemblance to the 928 which would have a heavier V-8 and couldn't be rear-engined.

Once the front location was picked, Porsche engineers decided to mount the transmission at the rear to create as equal as possible front/rear weight distribution (it came out 48 front, 52 rear). The rear transmission location also resulted in a high polar moment of inertia which is a near-ideal safety factor because, although a car of this type isn't quite as agile as a mid-engined car with its inherent low polar moment, it is easier for the average-to-good driver to handle in all circumstances. A car with low polar moment

117

is difficult to "catch" once it starts to spin, for example, whereas a car with high polar moment is more forgiving; a factor that would be appreciated by old Porsche hands.

The new design had already been guaranteed an independent rear suspension, so mounting the transmission at the back in unit with the differential became only a matter of mechanical problem solving. Besides, Porsche management liked the transaxle idea because it was "technically interesting" and that was considered important for a Porsche.

The 1984 cc single-overhead-camshaft cast-iron-block engine was just over-square with a bore of 86.5 mm and a stroke of 84.4 mm. The aluminum crossflow cylinder head had 9.3:1 compression ratio (8:1 U.S.) and Heron-type chambers, which meant that the piston crowns were dished and the head surface was flat.

A Bosch K-Jetronic CIS fuel injection system fed into 40 mm inlet valves (38 mm U.S.) with 12 mm lift, and exited through 33 mm exhaust valves with 11.8 mm lift. Double valve springs were used on all valves and the exhaust valves rotated during lift for better cooling and wear characteristics. The toothed belt-driven camshaft turned in five plain bearings and operated the valves through cup-type tappets.

As on all Porsches after the 356 series, the electrical system was 12-volt, and the European 924 had a conventional ignition system

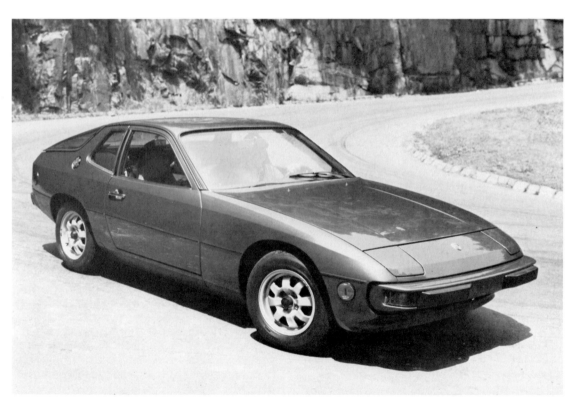

The first 924 came off the assembly line in November 1975, as a 1976 model in Europe, but the first 924 to reach the U.S. market in April 1976 was called a 1977 model. It differed from the European version with large, round side-marker lights front and rear, and bumpers protruding more to meet U.S. safety requirements.

The headlights were raised by a rotating shaft operated by an electric motor. The 924 Turbo body had the best drag coefficient of any European production car, at .034C$_d$, but the 924 shape didn't impress customers the way a new Porsche should. *Porsche+Audi*

but the U.S. version used transistor-type breakerless ignition. The engine was installed at an angle of forty degrees from vertical, to the right. The alternator, exhaust and spark plugs were on the right side with the intake on the left. This would normally be immaterial, but inasmuch as the engine was tilted to the right, this was also the low side and made spark plug changing an adventure.

The engine, with its cast-iron block, although considered a VW design, was fully developed and tested at Audi Research in Ingolstadt. All 924 engines for the United States had exhaust-gas recirculation, and the forty-nine-state cars had air injection while the California cars had catalytic converters. After development at Audi, the engine was built at VW's Salzgitter plant. As delivered to Porsche it weighed 300 pounds.

Power rating for the European version was 125 DIN/119 SAE net 5800 rpm, with a compression ratio of 9.3:1. In the form in which it would go to the United States it produced 100 DIN/95.4 SAE at 5500 rpm with 8.0:1 compression ratio. When the automatic transmission was introduced, the U.S. version was rated at 115 DIN/110 SAE net at 5750, with a compression ratio of 8.5:1.

Drive went through a single-plate, diaphragm-spring clutch, mounted at the back of the engine. The driveshaft, 20 mm in diameter, revolved inside an 85-mm-diameter steel torque tube which tied the engine rigidly to the transaxle assembly at the rear. The transmission, when the car was first introduced, was a four-speed unit with a cone-type synchromesh—the first Porsche since the early nonsynchro 356 that didn't use Porsche's patented synchromesh system. Because of the high rotating inertia of the driveshaft, the synchromesh cones were sprayed with molybdenum to prevent excessive wear.

The transaxle was from the 1972 and later Audis, installed in a Porsche-designed aluminum die-cast housing. The half-shafts were from the Volkswagen Type 181 "Thing" and ran at an angle of ten degrees rearward to the hubs.

Front suspension was a combination of Volkswagen parts—coil spring MacPherson shock strut from the Beetle, and lower A-arms from the Rabbit/Golf/Scirocco. These lower arms were the same, left and right. The front end suspension geometry was designed with negative roll radius (the center line of the wheel's pivot axis intersected the ground slightly outside the center of the front tire's contact patch). Steering was the rack and pinion from the Rabbit, but with 19.4:1 ratio instead of the 17.4:1 of the Rabbit.

At the rear, transverse torsion bars 22 mm in diameter were connected to flat steel trailing links and suspension arms pivoted off the tubular torsion bar housing. Front shocks were from the VW Beetle, and either Boge or Fichtel & Sachs units were used at the rear. Anti-roll bars, 20 mm front and 18 mm rear, were options at the beginning. Brakes, too, were VW—Beetle solid disc at the front, K-70 drums at the rear, with a dual diagonal system vacuum-boosted.

The suspension was attached to a unit-body that was unique to the 924 which, once more, followed Porsche's established tradition with all its previous cars.

Body design was dictated to some degree by the previously mentioned parameters of the basic concept, but details were debated strongly among Porsche management. Some thought the car should have a grille at the front, others preferred to follow Porsche's grilleless tradition even though the new car would be water-cooled. The latter won out, and air was taken in under the front bumper—conceding the necessity to have a family resemblance to the 356 and 911.

The body design was created by Dutchman Harm Lagaay of the Porsche design office and finalized by the design staff. The body in final form had a frontal area of 18.95 square feet (slightly more than the 911) but had a Cd (aerodynamic drag coefficient) of 0.36, making it one of the best in the world at that time. The 924 Turbo has a Cd of 0.34 which is the best in Europe as of this writing. But I'm ahead of the story.

An electric motor raised and lowered the headlights. U.S. cars had aluminum bumpers—castings in front, extrusions at the back—attached to hydraulic energy absorbers. The U.S. cars also had round side-marker lights to conform to American regulations.

The VW/Audi engine in the 924 used Bosch CIS fuel injection. Single overhead camshaft was driven by toothed belt.

The instrument panel contained three dials: center, speedometer; right, 8000 rpm tachometer; and left, fuel, water temperature and warning lights. All three were covered with conical glass as an antiglare measure. The driver sat in 911 seats, covered in cloth, vinyl or optional leather, and looked at the instruments through a steering wheel that was offset about one-half inch above center to give added leg clearance.

Such was the 924 as it was first conceived. Before production began, however, problems within almost kept it from production. In 1973, the VG was disbanded, and the design became VW property inasmuch as it had been financed by VW. Then-VW director Rudolph Leiding wanted it for VW or Audi because he saw the advantage of marketing

Aerodynamic efficiency and cargo space dictated the shape of the rear, but it was one of the least appealing views of the 924. The rear window wiper was part of the Touring Package II for the U.S. market in 1977. The rear window/hatchback lifted for luggage stowage and access. *Porsche+Audi*

it through the 2,000 VW dealers in West Germany instead of the 200 VW-Porsche dealers that had been established to market the 914.

Then a seemingly unrelated matter added fuel to Porsche's fire—the OPEC oil embargo of 1973-74 caused Leiding to have second thoughts about an upgraded car for VW. Late in 1974 Leiding was asked to leave Volkswagen and Toni Schmucker came into top position at VW in February 1975.

Schmucker, a former Ford executive, wanted to close one of VW's eight plants, and chose the old NSU facility at Neckarsulm as the one to go. Things were beginning to go Porsche's way now, and as a result of these and other factors Porsche and VW agreed to build the new 924 at the Neckarsulm plant, using the same workforce that had been there under NSU and, later, VW management.

Production was planned for 100 cars per day when the first 924s came off the assembly line in November 1975. By April 1976, it had reached sixty cars per day and the first production models reached U.S. dealers in April, as 1977 models.

In 1976, West German models were sold for DM 23,240 ($8,900), and the base price of the 1977 model in the United States was $9,395. The optional removable roof panel was $330; air conditioning, $548; front and rear anti-roll bars, $105; metallic paint, $295; and three radio speakers and antenna, $105. The American models were designed to meet all U.S. air pollution standards.

Touring Package I, consisting of triple speakers, leather-covered steering wheel and six-inch-wide alloy road wheels for 185/70 HR-14 radials, was $345. Touring Package II, with headlight washers, rear window wiper and right-hand outside mirror, was another $240.

In February 1977, the engine was improved for the U.S. market; the compression ratio was raised to 8.5:1, a new camshaft with the timing advanced seven degrees, and 40 mm intake valves increased the horsepower to 110 SAE net at 5750 rpm. At the same time the rear axle ratio was changed from 3.44 to 3.88:1. They were "fifty-state" cars and all had catalytic converters for emissions control.

A three-speed automatic transmission, the first in Porsche's history, became an option on European 924s in late 1976, and on U.S. cars in March 1977. The rear axle ratio was 3.455:1 in Europe and 3.727 for the United States.

At the Frankfurt show in 1977, Porsche introduced the long-awaited five-speed transmission as an option for the 924. Unfortunately, it was the "Getrag" shift pattern with second, third, fourth and fifth in the normal H pattern, with first off to the left and below reverse. The five-speed was accompanied by a rear axle ratio change from 3.444 to 4.714:1. The difference is not quite as much as it seems because of simultaneous changes in the transmission gears. Remember, all gears are indirect in the 924 transmission, and both fourth and fifth are "overdrive" in relation to the ring and pinion ratio.

Performance of the 1978 model 924 was little changed from before, but the flexibility of the five-speed made it a much more enjoyable car to drive, and economy was increased measurably. Coupled with improvements in suspension attachment that decreased road noise, the 924 was finally becoming the car Porsche had wanted it to be.

Porsche of Great Britain worked out a deluxe package for its market that included alloy wheels, headlamp washers and rear window wiper and tinted glass, all included in the base price.

For 1979, the five-speed was made standard, with the three-speed automatic still an option. The abominable space-saver spare was utilized (except in England where it was illegal) to give slightly more luggage space, and pressure-cast alloy wheels, tinted glass, vanity mirror on the sun visor and stereo speakers were included as standard equipment.

The big news for 1979, however, was the addition of a turbocharged version which could be identified by the four air intakes just above the front bumper, the NACA intake duct on the right side of the hood, its own unique alloy wheels, rear gravel guards and spoilers—a "chin" spoiler at the lower front of the car, and a "ducktail" at the rear of the deck lid.

With the rear seatback folded flat, a surprising amount of gear can be carried, but it's still no station wagon. *Greg Brown/Argus*

Steering wheel rim of the 924 was not concentric with hub (offset toward the top), for better instrument visibility and more leg room. It was still a tight fit, and got worse as the wheel turned.

A Championship Edition 924 was offered in February 1977, to commemorate Porsche's winning the 1976 World Championship of Makes. This special edition of 2,000 cars came in one trim: all-white body with red, white and blue side stripes; white alloy wheels; red corduroy seats with blue piping; red carpeting in both passenger and luggage areas; leather-covered steering wheel; and anti-roll bars front and rear. *Porsche+Audi*

Inside, a three-spoke, leather-covered steering wheel (like the 911 Turbo) and leather boot for the shift linkage were the quick identifying features. There was no boost gauge, as Porsche engineers thought it unnecessary. European 924 Turbos had four-wheel disc brakes, while the U.S. Turbos still had the disc-front, drum-rear of the standard 924. A sport package option for any 1979 924 included the four-wheel disc brakes of the European Turbo.

The major changes brought about in creating the 924 Turbo were mechanical, even though the cosmetic changes were the most obvious. The "short-blocks" (cylinder block, crankshaft, connecting rods and pistons) were the same on both 924 and Turbo, and these were assembled at Neckarsulm on the same assembly line. But before final assembly, the Turbo short-blocks were trucked to Porsche's Zuffenhausen works where final assembly was to take place adding other components unique to the Turbo.

After checking what had been assembled, a new cylinder head with recessed combustion chambers was installed. Using a "flattened hemisphere" chamber coupled with the dished pistons gave a "flattened spherical" chamber and a compression ratio of 7.5:1. Spark plugs (platinum tipped) were moved to the intake side of the head, and water seal between block and head was accomplished by a copper gasket and silicone rings.

CIS fuel injection was standard on the Turbo just as it was on the normally-aspi-

In February 1977, horsepower of the 924 was increased from 95 to 110 on U.S. models—all of which were "50 state" cars with catalytic converters for emission control. At this time the first fully automatic transmission ever offered in Porsche became an option. The model was designated a 1977½ in the United States. *Porsche+Audi*

123

The 924 interior was state-of-the-art design in 1977, but for some reason the overall package appealed more to new Porsche buyers than it did to previous owners. And in 1979 the 924 accounted for 60 percent of Porsche's production (including 911 and 928). In March 1979, Porsche sold more cars in Germany than it did in the United States for the first time. *Porsche + Audi*

rated 924, but two fuel pumps were utilized to ensure full pressure maintenance under all driving conditions. The new pump was submerged in the fuel tank, and subsequently became the standard pump for both models, as a production economy.

The KKK (Kuhnle, Kopp & Kausch) Turbocharger was fitted to the exhaust manifold, and the system contained a wastegate downstream from the exhaust manifold. Including a wastegate provided pressure regulation, and also protected the catalytic converter from an overload of extremely high exhaust temperatures. Mounting the turbocharger on the right side required relocation of the starter to the left side of the engine.

The driveshaft was enlarged from a 20 to 25 mm diameter to handle the extra horsepower, and only a five-speed transmission

Visual changes through 1981 were so minor as to be almost unnoticeable. In 1980, the 924 had received a new transmission with the five-speed shift pattern in the more "normal" H (the first four speeds and fifth up to the right beside third), although the Turbo retained the Getrag pattern (with the four top gears in the H and first down and to the left). The lower body shell was covered by a limited rust-perforation warranty of six years. Four-wheel disc brakes became standard for all 924 models in 1981. *Porsche+ Audi*

could be obtained with the turbocharged engine.

In turbocharged form, the European-market engine produced 170 DIN horsepower at 5500 rpm, with 180 foot-pounds of torque at 3500 rpm. The rear axle ratio was 4.125 for European specification cars. The U.S. version was rated at 143 SAE horsepower at 5500 with 147 foot-pounds of torque at 3000 rpm, and the axle ratio was 4.71:1.

Because the Turbo engine was sixty-four pounds heavier than the standard 924 unit, some suspension changes were in order—recalibrated front springs, heavier anti-roll bar in front (and a slightly smaller one at the rear) and stiffer shocks. The rear track was widened by 0.8 inch. Weight distribution changed from 48/52 of the standard 924, to 49/51 for the Turbo (empty) or 44/56 with passengers and fuel.

For 1980, the 924 received a new transmission—a five-speed with a normal shift pattern, which was arranged by adding a fifth gear to the old four-speed assembly. The Turbo retained the five-speed with the Getrag shift pattern, as the 924's modified four-speed couldn't handle the torque of the turbo engine.

The lower body shell of both 924 and 924 Turbo was now covered by a limited rust perforation warranty for six years.

The basic car, both normal and Turbo, remained unchanged for 1981, but four-wheel disc brakes became standard for all versions—largely because of customer complaints. All models received halogen lights and rear seat belts. Other minor changes continued to be made when Porsche management thought them to be necessary. Nothing is ever static at Porsche.

Since the introduction of the first 924, customer complaints revolved around engine roughness, too much interior noise for a car of this price class, poor ventilation (U.S. owners were more insistent on air conditioning than European or British customers), rather plain interior (again, for price class), choppy ride, vibrations that shook screws out of the dash, electric options that caused more than ordinary trouble and, in American models, poor performance.

On the other side of the coin, customers and magazine road testers praised handling, brakes (except for the disc/drums on early U.S. Turbos), space, looks and general assembly quality. Given the above pros and

Rear ducktail spoiler, modest rear-wheel mud flaps were standard on the 924 Turbo. Button in left rear corner of backlight covered hole where optional rear window wiper would be attached. *Author*

The 924 Turbo engine with its KKK (Kuhnle, Kopp & Kausch) turbocharger produced the sort of performance the 924 should have had in the first place for the U.S. market. *Author*

cons, it's unfortunate that the 924 will automatically be compared to other Porsches. On its own, and standing by itself, it's not a bad car. The pluses outweigh the minuses and, if built by another manufacturer would probably be rated higher in the automotive enthusiast's mind than it is being a Porsche.

Production of the 924 and 924 Turbo ended, for the export market, at the end of 1981,but continued for the home market, where engine size determined taxes to be paid on the car each year.

The 924 Turbo was a bit of a disappointment: Porsche didn't like the sales figures, and the customers didn't like the performance, which was coupled with expensive maintenance costs. The 924 Turbo is already a rare car, which does not make it a valuable collector item! Another fairly rare 924 is the Sebring Special Edition, which was primarily a striped and trimmed version, but a few

were made with suspension and brake changes for would-be racers. Those too, are not particularly good investments for speculators.

In June 1986 the 924 reappeared on the U.S. market as the 924S. The body was the same as before, but the engine, drive train, brakes, suspension and electrical system were from the 944. Standard equipment included air conditioning, tinted glass, electrically adjustable and heated outside mirrors (left and right), power steering, power windows, antenna, four speakers, convenience package including anti-theft wheels, and coin and cassette holders. Optional equipment included AM/FM stereo radio and cassette tape player, electric sunroof, automatic transmission, limited-slip differential and a rear window wiper.

The 924S claimed a top speed of 134 miles per hour, 0-60 in 8.3 seconds with the five-

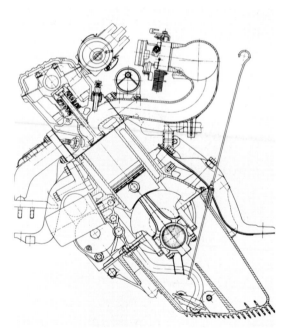

Front view of the 924 engine—which is slanted 40 degrees to the right from vertical—in cross section shows the overhead camshaft operating on cups over the valvestems, and the flat cylinder head surface (the chamber is in the top of the piston), deep oil pan for the wet-sump lubrication system. *Porsche+Audi*

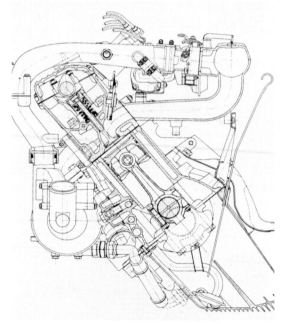

Cross section of the 924 Turbo engine is basically that of the 924 but with the turbo unit on the lower side to pick up the exhaust close to the ports. The intake goes from there up and over the valve cover to a plenum chamber on the intake side of the engine and through individual pipes to each intake port. *Porsche+Audi*

speed manual and 9.8 with the three-speed automatic transmission.

This model was brought back to the U.S. market as an "entry-level" Porsche, with a price of $19,900, which went up to $21,900 in November 1986. Compared to other car prices in 1987, that was still a bargain price, and particularly so for a Porsche. Unfortunately, this "entry level" Porsche is no more—production stopped on the 924 at the end of 1988. So far, this hasn't seemed to affect prices on used 924 models, and we don't forecast their prices rising steeply in the near future.

Front engine, rear transmission in unit with the axle, connected by a torque-tube driveshaft. A four-speed all-synchromesh transmission was used exclusively until a three-speed fully automatic transmission became optional on European 924s in late 1976, and for the U.S. market in March, 1977. The five-speed transmission became an option after the Frankfurt auto show in 1977. *Porsche+Audi*

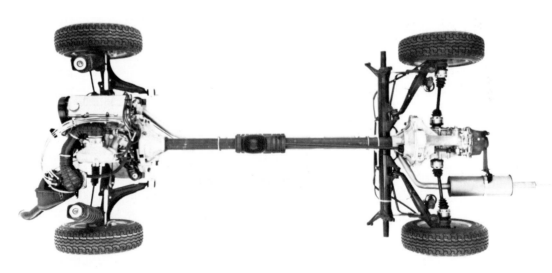

The 1977 924 chassis layout shows the Audi transmission at the back which was used through 1978, was replaced for 1979 by the Porsche-designed gearbox, and then came back into use in 1980 and is still used on the 924, 924 Turbo and 944. The half-shafts trail toward the rear at a 10-degree angle. *Porsche+Audi*

The 1980 924 Turbo chassis design, with the Porsche transmission which was used in the 924 in 1979, and the Turbo in 1980 only. The 924 and 924 Turbo (for Europe) and the 944 now use the Audi unit exclusively. The half-shafts, for this layout, lead toward the front by a 10-degree angle. The rear suspension and mounting shown here was adopted in 1978 for both the 924 and 924 Turbo, and was carried into the 944 design. *Porsche+Audi*

For 1981, the 924 Turbo got the standard shift pattern of the 924 and 911SC, four-wheel disc brakes as standard equipment and a modified turbocharger to give better response. The Turbo can be identified by the four air intakes above the bumper and the NACA duct on the right side of the hood. *Porsche+Audi*

924 & 924 Turbo

Engine
Design: .... Water-cooled inline four
Borexstroke, mm/inches: 86.5x84.4/3.41x3.32
Displacement, cc/cubic inches: 1984/121.06
Valve operation: 914 ...... Toothed belt-driven single overhead camshaft
Compression ratio: Europe & Great Britain 9.3:1
   U.S., Canada, California, Japan
    (manual transmission) 8.0:1
   U.S., Canada, California, Japan
    (automatic transmission) 8.5:1
   Turbo (from 1979) 7.5:1
Carburetion: 924 .... Bosch K-Jetronic fuel injection
   924 Turbo .... Exhaust-driven turbocharger & Bosch K-Jetronic fuel injection
BHP (Mfr): Europe & Great Britain .... 125 DIN/119 SAE @ 5800
   U.S., Canada, California, Japan
    (manual transmission) .... 100 DIN/95.4 SAE @ 5500
   U.S., Canada, California, Japan
    (automatic transmission) .... 115 DIN/110 SAE @ 5750
   Turbo (from 1979) .... 150 DIN/143 SAE @ 5500

Chassis & drivetrain
Frame: .... Unit body
Component layout: .... Front engine, rear drive
Clutch: .... Fichtel & Sachs single dry-plate
Transmission: .... Porsche five-speed, all-synchromesh, in unit with differential
Optional three-speed automatic, in unit with differential
Axle ratio: California, Canada, Japan
   with four-speed manual transmission 3.89:1
   Europe and rest of world
   with four-speed manual transmission 3.44:1
   U.S., California, Canada, Japan
   with three-speed automatic transmission 3.73:1
   Europe and rest of world
   with three-speed automatic transmission 3.45:1
Rear suspension: .... Independent, semi-trailing arms, transverse torsion bars & tubular shock absorbers (anti-roll bar optional)
Front suspension: .... Independent, MacPherson telescopic shock strut & lower A-arm on each side with coil springs (anti-roll bar optional)

General
Wheelbase, mm/inches: 2400/94.5
Track, front, mm/inches: 1481/55.8
   rear, mm/inches: 1372/54.0
Brakes: .... Disc front, drum rear (all-disc optional)
Tire size, front & rear: .... 165 HR 14
   (185/70 HR 14 with optional wheels)
Wheels: .... 5½Jx14 steel (6Jx14 alloy optional)
Body builder: .... Porsche or Karmann

The 924 Turbo op-art interior, standard on the first 600 sent to the United States, is more comfortable physically than it is visually and, fortunately, the driver can see little of the black and white checkered flag look while seated in the car. *Bill Appleton/Argus*

The engine and drivetrain, brakes and electrical system of the 924S are taken directly from the 944 with minimal modifications to suit the chassis. The 147-horsepower engine gives the 924S a top speed of 134 mph and 0–60 in 8.3 seconds with the manual five-speed transmission.

The 924S was re-introduced in 1986 as a 1987
model. It is the low-priced Porsche and is an
excellent entry-level car for those who want
Porsche quality and performance.

924S

Engine
Design: .... Water-cooled inline four
Borexstroke, mm/inches: 100x78.9/3.94x3.11
Displacement, cc/cubic inches: 2479/151
Valve operation: .... Toothed belt-driven single overhead
  camshaft
Compression ratio: 9.7:1
Carburetion: .... Bosch DME fuel injection
BHP (Mfr): .... 147 @ 5800

Chassis & drivetrain
Frame: .... Unit body
Component layout: .... Front engine, rear drive
Clutch: .... Fichtel & Sachs single dry-plate
Transmission: (standard) .... Porsche five-speed,
                                   all-synchromesh,
  (optional) .... Porsche three-speed automatic
                               in unit with differential

Axle ratio: (manual) 3.89:1
  (automatic) 3.46:1
Rear suspension: .... Independent, semi-trailing arms,
  transverse torsion bars & tubular shock absorbers
Front suspension: .... Independent, MacPherson telescopic
  shock strut & lower A-arm on each side with coil springs

General
Wheelbase, mm/inches: 2400/94.5
Track, front, mm/inches: 1419/55.9
  rear, mm/inches: 1393/54.8
Brakes: .... Hydraulic, dual-circuit system,
  4 ventilated disc, brake servo
Tire size, front & rear: .... 195/65 HR 15
Wheels: .... 6J–15 cast alloy
Body builder: .... Porsche

Chapter 11

928

There is a game played by Porsche enthusiasts, automotive writers and Porsche management, and it goes like this: Question (from enthusiasts or writers): "How long will you continue to build the 911?" Answer (from Porsche management): "As long as there is a demand for the model."

So far the answer has proven to be correct, and it looks as though the 911 may go on for a long time. But, secretly, Porsche management had been concerned for many years that the demand would not only drop off, but it might do it so suddenly that it could catch them unprepared with no replacement. Never fear. It didn't happen, and it won't happen.

In the early 1970s the Porsche men were considering a new car—one that would not only serve as a suitable replacement for the 911 when the time came, but one which would be in tune with the 1980s. The new car would have to have all the quality and performance of previous Porsches, but it also would have to be capable of meeting any and all government regulations that might be conceived in the foreseeable future.

Porsche, at that time, was under the direction of Dr. (later Prof.) Ernst Fuhrmann. When interviewed by Karl Ludvigsen for his book *Porsche: Excellence Was Expected*, Fuhrmann recalled the new car's concept was "worked out, deliberated, and decided within a few days." This first-ever Porsche to be designed from a clean sheet of paper as an all-Porsche car would have a water-cooled front engine, transmission and differential combined in a rear transaxle, all-independent suspension and disc brakes. Those were the major technical parameters. The means of achieving the goals would come as the engineering team developed the design.

Fuhrmann wanted a large-enough engine to deliver power beyond the 911's potential (without resorting to supercharging), but also one that was quieter in operation. A large-displacement engine was considered essential not only for the car's performance and image, but to be able to meet expected legislative handicaps placed on engines to make them emission free.

A sixty-degree V-6 was considered, but rejected in favor of a ninety-degree V-8. A V-8 would satisfy all the requirements outlined by Fuhrmann; it had more than adequate power potential, a V-8 has good balance and is therefore inherently smooth, it would fit under the sloping hood he wanted to carry on the Porsche styling tradition, and it would have room for more displacement if later desired.

The decision to mount the engine in front, and the transmission at the back in unit with the differential, was based on the desire to obtain near-equal weight distribution front and rear. But there were other reasons too: This arrangement provided a high polar moment of inertia which aided handling, and a high measure of safety for all driver levels. Less obvious, but no less important, were the factors that a front-engined car could usually pass crash tests more easily than a rear-engined car, and the longer exhaust system allowed more room for mufflers and catalytic converters if needed.

Because the United States has absorbed approximately fifty percent of all Porsches ever produced, the American market has to be considered by Porsche when designing a new car. Unfortunately, it is impossible to anticipate how far and which direction American bureaucratic ingenuity will take these regulations. And Porsche management also realizes that safety and emission controls in force in America might well be copied by other countries sometime in the future.

After all the preliminary work had been done, the final go or no-go decision was to be made in 1973 and the timing couldn't have been worse—it coincided with OPEC's oil embargo. The same situation that was to drive the 924 from VW/Audi back into Porsche's waiting arms (see previous chapter)as a truly economical sports/GT car could now stop, or postpone, the new V–8 luxury Porsche. We'll never know what agony Porsche management went through, but it decided to go ahead with the new car.

That decision was a major corporate gamble, and took great courage. Porsche had to count on a near-future relief from the oil shortage, and that public opinion, four or five years hence when the new car would be introduced, would accept a relatively thirsty and seemingly ostentatious car. Admittedly, in the quantities that would be produced, this was a safer gamble than it would have been for Ford or Chevrolet.

Porsche chose the Geneva Salon in March 1977, as the debut for the new 928. The first Porsche 356 had been presented to the public at Geneva in 1950, but since that time the new models, or major changes, were introduced at the bi-annual Frankfurt show which is traditionally held in September of odd years.

It was a dazzling creation that was shown to an appreciative show crowd at Geneva; different from anything seen from Porsche before, and different from anything else on the road or at the show from any other manufacturer. It had seemed to be almost a law in Germany (unwritten, and maybe more subliminal than actual) that Volkswagen built economy cars, Opel and Ford covered the middle ground, Mercedes-Benz built luxury sedans (almost unchallenged until BMW got into the act), and Porsche built sports cars. Now here was Porsche invading the Mercedes-Benz/BMW territory in grand style.

When introduced at the Geneva auto show in March 1977, the Porsche 928 was viewed as a daring departure from Porsche philosophy. The water-cooled 4.5-liter V–8 was mounted in the front, driving the rear wheels through a five-speed transaxle (three-speed automatic optional). In true Porsche tradition, however, all four wheels were independently sprung, and great attention was paid to aerodynamics. This was later to prove an embarrassment as the C_d was no better than many family sedans, and not as good as that of the 924T—which is the best in Europe as of this writing. *Porsche+Audi*

The all-new 928 was conceived to be a grand tourer in the most grand manner, with all the luxury, passenger convenience and comfort features any reasonable owner could ever want. You couldn't get a TV or wet-bar, but those are only for stretched limos used to haul rock stars from airport to hotel.

Porsche engineers, as would be expected, didn't forget more important items such as handling and safety. The 928 was as good underneath the skin (better, actually) as it was on the outside.

Power was supplied by a ninety-degree V–8, with 95 mm bore and 78.9 mm stroke, giving a displacement of 4474 cc (273 cubic inches). The cylinder block and heads were cast of Reynolds 390 aluminum alloy, which required no liners in the cylinder bores. A single overhead camshaft on each bank was driven by a toothed Gilmer-type belt.

Fuel (premium in Europe, unleaded in the United States) was supplied from the 86–liter (22.7-U.S.-gallon) plastic tank at the extreme rear of the car, via an electric pump submerged in the tank. Disbursement to each cylinder was provided by a Bosch K-Jetronic injection system (CIS). Horsepower, of the U.S. version, was rated at 230 DIN and 219 SAE net at 5250 rpm, while the European and English models produced 240 DIN and 229 SAE net horsepower at 5500 rpm.

Drive went through a Fichtel & Sachs double-disc clutch that was only 200 mm (7.875 inches) in diameter, and a 25–mm–diameter solid-steel driveshaft running inside a 100–mm–diameter torque tube to the rear-mounted transmission. A three-speed automatic—actually the inner works of the Mercedes-Benz 6.9 automatic transmission—with torque converter, could be ordered. With this option, there was a starter ring gear at the engine, but no flywheel. A 2.75:1 set of differential gears transferred the power to short half-shafts, each with inner and outer constant-velocity U-joints.

Unlike the transaxle of the 924, the transmission of the 928 was mounted ahead of the differential, and was more like a transmission found in a "normal" front-engined, rear-drive car. All Porsches prior to the 928 had indirect gears on all speeds, with the driveshaft lining up with a secondary shaft in the transmission. The driveshaft of the 928 was in line with the upper main shaft which was linked directly to the pinion gear in the differential. One advantage to this layout was the resultant quieter operation which was one of the original goals for the 928.

Unfortunately, the Porsche men chose the once-discarded shift pattern for the five-speed which had second, third, fourth and fifth in the H pattern, and first off to the left below the reverse slot. Part of their reasoning was that the V–8 produced enough torque that first gear was not normally needed once the engine was warmed up, and wouldn't falter when starting in second.

To cope with the available power, and to give the best combination of handling and ride comfort, an entirely new suspension was created for the 928. They did call on previous experience from the racing 804 (1962 GP car) and 904, however.

Front suspension consisted of parallel but unequal-length A-arms on each side, with a concentric tubular shock absorber and coil spring attached to the lower A-arm and passing through the upper arm to its chassis attachment point at the top. The front-wheel pivot axis intersected the ground just outside the center of the tire patch contact center, resulting in negative steering roll radius. The car was steered by a power-assisted ZF rack and pinion mounted behind the front wheel center line.

A new rear suspension, Porsche called it the "Weissach axle" in honor of the Porsche research and development center where the axle was created, was one of the unique features of the 928, and one of which Porsche engineering seemed most proud. Probably with just cause.

It is difficult to explain but, briefly, a single upper arm on each side was mounted laterally—from frame to hub—while each lower arm pivoted at an angle from its mounting points on the chassis forward of the axle, in effect, a semi-trailing arm. The advantage, aside from creating a fully independent suspension, was that of suspension geometry. During cornering, if power was reduced or

From the rear the American 928 differed from its
European counterpart by the addition of running lights and rubber bumper inserts around
the license molding. *Porsche+Audi and Porsche
Werkfoto*

brakes applied, the outside rear wheel toed inward instead of outward as on other independent rear suspension designs. This helped prevent the rear of the car from sliding further outward (oversteer) which tended to either put the car off the road backward, or direct it into the inside of the curve.

Springs at the rear were concentric with the tubular shock absorbers, as at the front, and a smaller 21 mm anti-roll bar was fitted.

Ventilated disc brakes were used all around, operated by dual diagonal brake circuits. The hand brake actuated small brake shoes inside drums in the rear discs; a system used by Porsche since the 356C in 1965. Carrying on another Porsche tradition, the running gear was attached to a unit body of welded sheet steel construction which had been galvanized to prevent rust perforation-guaranteed for seven years. Pursuant to Porsche's goals to use as much light metal, and plastic, as possible to save weight, the doors, front fenders and engine hood were made of a special aluminum alloy. Energy-absorbing bumpers, front and rear, were covered with polyurethane caps which were faired into the body.

Driver convenience and comfort were of the highest order, and established the state of the art for the time. An adjustable steering wheel (up and down) had the distinction of being accompanied by the instrument cluster when it was raised or lowered, keeping the instruments in constant view of whatever-size driver sat behind the wheel.

In addition, there were power windows, central locking system, air conditioning (which cooled the glove compartment as well as the interior), cruise control, four-speaker stereo, rear window wiper with two-stage electric defogger, retractable headlights and headlight washers, electrically adjusted and heated outside rearview mirror, illuminated vanity mirror and sun visors for the rear seat passengers.

A console-mounted central warning system monitored fluid levels, lights and brake pad wear. A light in the center of the instrument cluster warned of any major problem in the car. The suggested retail price of the 928 (U.S.) was $26,000.

Optional equipment included an electrically operated sunroof, limited-slip differen-tial, right-hand outside mirror, leather interior and an alarm system activated by a special-cut, longer door key.

The 928 was the largest Porsche built, but its 2+2 seating was fit into a body with only 0.4-inch more wheelbase than a Corvette (98.4 to 98). It weighed less than the Vette (3,197 to 3,534 pounds) and the body length was even ten inches shorter (175.7 to 185.2). The two back seats were not something one would want to ride in across the country, but for short distances the car offered genuine seating for four.

Porsche had expected to gain most of its 928 customers from conquest sales, rather than its own customers moving up. As it turned out, during the first year of sales sixty percent went to new Porsche owners and forty percent of the cars were in the hands of previous Porsche owners. The new Porsche owners loved the 928, the old Porsche pushers didn't. The latter group seemed to expect the 928 to be just like their last Porsche—but more so—when, in fact, it was an entirely different automobile.

The quality was there, the handling was there, the performance was there, but the Old Porsche Feel wasn't there. And it wasn't there for a good reason: Porsche didn't

The op-art interiors of the first 928s didn't impress the viewers and elicited more sarcasm than praise. It was not one of Porsche's better designs. *Porsche+Audi*

Power for the 928 was furnished by a V–8 engine with cylinder block and heads made of Reynolds 390 aluminum alloy. Displacement was 273 cubic inches (4474 cc), and fuel was metered to the engine by a Bosch electronically controlled AFC fuel injection. A toothed, belt-driven single camshaft on each bank operated the in-line valves. Horsepower rating at this writing is 231 DIN U.S. and 240 DIN in Europe and England. *Porsche Werkfoto*

intend it to be like other Porsches. It would be a car for the 1980s and the 1990s. If the 356 series could survive for fifteen years, and the type 911 for twelve (at the time of the 928 introduction; and at this writing, twenty years with no end in sight), then the 928 could take Porsche into the twenty-first century. It began to look as though maybe Porsche management didn't see this as a replacement for the 911 after all. They now had a "low-priced" 924, a "mid-priced" 911, and a high-priced 928; four, six and V–8 cylinders, water-cooled, air-cooled, front engine and rear engine.

That, too, was in keeping with Porsche philosophy. It wasn't stated openly, but Fuhrmann admitted that Porsche wanted to bring a water-cooled engine and new chassis design to a similar state of perfection that had been accomplished with the rear-engined air-cooled cars. Aside from a conviction that the 928 engine and chassis layout was the way to go, it could serve as a notice to prospective customers that Porsche engineering could provide something other than an air-cooled engine mounted in the rear of the chassis.

Headlights were raised on the 928 by an electric motor and a shaft common to both lights. American versions included high and low beam in one light. European models used pop-up lights for low-beam only, and had high-beam lights set into the front bumper. The black button in front of each headlight housed the nozzle for the headlight washer. *Porsche Werkfoto*

General specifications of the 928 remained the same through the first five years of production, but as with all Porsches, running changes were made to improve the car.

In 1980, several items that had been standard on 1979 U.S. cars were moved to the option list: 16x7–inch rims, radio and part-leather upholstery. Climate control, door warning light and electric sunroof were offered for the first time. A Sports Group, which included sixteen-inch wheels, firmer shock absorbers, spoilers and limited-slip differential, became a later option.

A 220–pound weight reduction was obtained by, among other things, using tubular steel for the pinion shaft, transmission main shaft and front anti-roll bar; and aluminum for the torque tube.

Engine changes included a rise in compression ratio (to 9.0:1 for U.S. cars, 10.0:1 for Europe and England), Bosch L-Jetronic fuel injection replaced the K-Jetronic for American models, valve overlap and lift were reduced, and the spark plug was moved 4 mm closer to the center of the combustion chamber. All this raised the horsepower of the U.S. 928 by *one*, but increased engine flexibility and economy—which was the goal.

The vacuum-operated door locks were replaced by electric locking, the air-conditioning system was improved, largely as a result of customer complaints. American buyers didn't like the brake squeal, but this wasn't a safety hazard (Porsche had always had excellent brakes, and those on the 928 were some of the best ever) so the company wasn't as quick to act on this as it was on other complaints.

In spite of being named the best sports car, or the best Grand Touring car, by most automotive magazines (or the best *car*, period, by some publications) the 928 was still not accepted as the best Porsche by Porsche enthusiasts. It had the potential for more power and more speed and, even if they couldn't use it, the die-hard Porsche enthusiasts wanted more.

Within a few months of the 924 Turbo introduction, the European Porsche buyer could get what he wanted: the 928S. Outside it was distinguished by the now-fashionable spoilers, new wheels and, to the careful observer, twin exhausts. Actually, the spoilers were more than just "joining the crowd" as they cleaned up the aerodynamics enough so the drag coefficient (C_d) got below 0.40

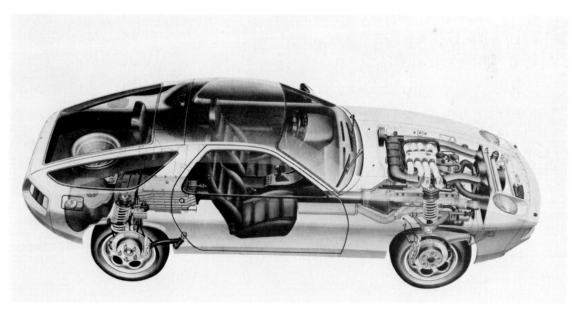

General component layout of the 928. *Porsche Werkfoto*

The 928 engine and clutch are connected to the rear transaxle by a torque tube. Unlike the 924, the 928 transmission is ahead of the rear axle, allowing the input to be in line with the transmission main shaft rather than on the lower, secondary shaft. Thus, it is like a normal transmission attached to the engine, but moved rearward. The 60 ampere-hour battery is mounted at the rear for better vehicle weight distribution, and is attached to the transaxle as a partial vibration dampener. Suspension is fully independent with coil springs, and anti-roll bars front and rear. *Porsche+Audi*

The very potent European 928S.

for the first time, at 0.38. The aerodynamics of the 928 had been an embarrassment to Porsche because, in spite of the jazzy look of the body, its drag coefficient had been no better than many sedans of the same period.

Underneath, mechanical changes increased the displacement to 4664 cc by virtue of a 2 mm bore increase. The larger bore was accompanied by better breathing, dual exhausts and 10:1 compression ratio; the result being 300 DIN horsepower at 5900 rpm. Top speed of the S was now 155 mph with a factory claim of 0-100 in 14.6 seconds. It was a fantastic achievement, especially considering the ease of driving the car. Its city manners were every bit as good as its high-speed road manners.

Inside, changes were minimal; a four-spoke steering wheel, better radio and a "blind" to cover the rear luggage compartment. To counterbalance the higher speed, thicker brake discs and larger brake pads were used on the S.

America had yet to see the 928S in legalized form, but as a sop to the American buyer who wanted to either have or boast about a better car, the 928 became available with a Competition Group accessory list. This included the spoilers of the 928 European S, Recaro seats, stiffer shock absorbers, padded steering wheel, limited-slip differential and 7Jx16 wheels. But no engine change. U.S. emissions rules killed that.

American customers finally got the real "S" in 1983; it was the only 928 offered in the U.S. market. A new four-speed automatic transmission—the insides by Daimler-Benz in a Porsche-designed case, as before—was now standard and the five-speed was optional.

Engine size was increased from 4474 to 4644 cc and the compression ratio went up to 9.3:1, producing 234 bhp at 5500 rpm. It was claimed to be the fastest, at 146 mph, street-legal car sold in the United States. Leather seats, electric window lifts, auto-

In 1981, a Competition Package 928 became available for the American market. With front and rear spoilers, leather interior, special shock absorbers and forged alloy wheels, the car had the look of the 928S (without the side trim strip, however), but not the performance. The American version would go nearly 140 mph even without the S engine tune; a respectable top speed. *Porsche+Audi*

matic climate control, electrically heated and actuated outside mirrors, and a handling package were standard.

The 928S went almost unchanged through 1984, but it really came of age in 1985, with the introduction of twin-cam cylinder heads with four valves per cylinder. The block was virtually the same as before, but with an extra three millimeters bore (up from 97.0 to 100 mm), which raised the displacement to 4957 cc (302 cu. in.). The compression ratio was also up, to 10.0:1, and the combination raised horsepower to 288 at 5750 rpm, and upped torque to 302 lb-ft at 2700 rpm.

A Bosch LH-Jetronic fuel injection with an air-mass flow meter was adopted, and the split four-cylinder ignitions were operated by a single unit for better control. The front port area of the three-way catalytic converter was increased by thirty-eight percent to reduce exhaust back pressure.

An already great car was getting better by the year, but with the penalty of a much higher price. The 928 was priced at $28,500 in 1979, $37,930 in 1980, $38,850 in 1982, $43,000 in 1983 (928S), $44,000 in 1984, $44,600 in 1985, and the 1986 928S 4 (the first in the United States with twin-cam heads) was $51,900 (source: *Road & Track* road test data panels).

The 928S was changed in subtle but important ways in 1986; the ABS braking system became standard, a windshield-contained radio antenna was introduced, and warranties were raised. The power train is now covered for five years or 50,000 miles; Porsche-built parts are covered for twelve months with unlimited mileage; and the rust-perforation coverage is up from seven to ten years.

For 1987, the 928S 4 (for fourth series of development, not for four camshafts), as it is now called, had some mechanical changes, primarily to engine induction, which raised horsepower to 316 SAE net at 6000 rpm. And a larger-diameter single disc clutch replaced the twin-disc unit. Two electronic knock sensors allowed the 928S 4 to run on a variety of unleaded fuels.

Outside, the body received the first real changes (other than spoilers and flares) since the 928 introduction. A new nose and front spoiler incorporated fog and driving lights and openings for engine and brake cooling. At the rear, new wraparound flush taillights and a "detached" spoiler helped both looks and aerodynamics. The coefficient of drag was 0.34, with virtually no lift at high speed and this, combined with the added power, gave the 928S 4 a claimed top speed of 165 mph with the five-speed manual, and 162 mph with the standard automatic transmission.

Porsche continues to call the 928 (the "S 4" appellation is dropped for 1990) its "Flag-

The steering wheel of the 928 didn't adjust in and out, but moved up and down—with the instrument cluster—to keep it in view of the driver at all times. The glovebox was air conditioned along with the interior. *Porsche+Audi*

ship" model, and rightly so. The 928 has more power, more top speed, more luxury, and more refinement than any other Porsche.

There were few, and only minor, changes for 1988 and 1989. This follows the "if-it-ain't-broke-don't fix-it" school of design and marketing and, while we understand there are some body changes coming we won't see them until at least 1991.

The list of standard equipment for the 928 would fill this page and there is little to aid comfort or convenience that has been left out—even the glovebox is air-conditioned.

For 1990 the power has been increased by 10 hp, up to 326 at 6200 rpm—but on the five-speed manual transmission models only. The four-speed automatic transmission-

equipped 928 continues with 316 hp, still at 6000 rpm.

Also included for 1990 is a limited-slip differential which automatically transfers torque between rear wheels as needed, according to wheel speed, wheel slip, and lateral acceleration. Revised shock absorber settings improve handling, and a 1990 addition is a tire pressure monitoring system which may be one of the best safety devices since shoulder harness/lap belts and anti-lock brake systems.

A display on the instrument panel alerts the driver by light and digital read-out when a tire is losing pressure and tells which tire it is. This is a derivation of the one used on the 959 Super Porsche.

But don't count the 928 as a "finished" car just yet. Porsche tradition has been to improve, upgrade, modify or change anything on a car if the engineers think it appropriate. The 928 engine has room to expand to 5.5 liters, and Fuhrmann's own 928 was turbo-charged, so *that* power-booster will fit.

---

928 (1978–82)
928S (1983–84)

Engine
Design: . . . . Water-cooled V-8
Borexstroke, mm/inches: 95x78.9/3.74x3.11; 97.0x78.9/3.82x3.11
Displacement, cc/cubic inches: 4474/273.0; 4644/285
Valve operation: . . . . Toothed belt-driven single overhead camshaft on each bank
Compression ratio: 1978–79 . . . . 8.5:1
1980–82 (U.S. & Japan) 9.0:1
1980–82 (Europe & England) 10.0:1
928S 9.3:1
Carburetion: 1978–82 (Europe) . . . . Bosch K-Jetronic fuel injection
1978–79 (U.S.) . . . . Bosch K-Jetronic fuel injection
1980–82 (U.S.) . . . . Bosch L-Jetronic fuel injection
BHP (Mfr): U.S. & Japan, 1978–79 . . . . 230 DIN/219 SAE @ 5250
Europe & England . . . . 240 DIN/229 SAE @ 5500
U.S. & Japan, 1980–82 . . . . 231 DIN/220 SAE @ 5500
928S . . . . 234 @ 5500
Chassis & drivetrain
Frame: . . . . Galvanized steel unitized
Component layout: . . . . Front engine, rear drive
Clutch: . . . . Fichtel & Sachs double dry-plate
Transmission: . . . . Porsche five-speed all-synchromesh (three-speed automatic optional); four-speed automatic (five-speed manual optional)
Rear suspension: . . . . Independent, upper transverse links, lower trailing arms, coil springs, tubular shock absorbers & anti-roll bar
Front suspension: . . . Independent, upper A-arms, lower trailing arms, coil springs, tubular shock absorbers & anti-roll bar
General
Wheelbase, mm/inches: 2500/98.4
Track, front, mm/inches: 1552/61.1
rear, mm/inches: 1530/60.2
Brakes: . . . . Ventilated disc
Tire size, front & rear: . . . . 225/50 VR 16 (215/60 VR 15 with automatic transmission)
Wheels: . . . Cast alloy 7Jx16 (7x15 with automatic transmission)
Body builder: . . . . Porsche

928S 4 (1985–)

Engine
Design: . . . . Water-cooled V-8
Borexstroke, mm/inches: 100.0x78.9/3.94x3.11
Displacement, cc/cubic inches: 4957/302
Valve operation: . . . . Toothed belt-driven twin overhead camshafts on each bank, four valves per cylinder
Compression ratio: 10.0:1
Carburetion: . . . . Bosch LH-Jetronic fuel injection
BHP (Mfr): 1985–86 . . . . 288 SAE net @ 5750
1987–89 . . . . 316 SAE net @ 6000
1990 . . . . 326 SAE net @ 6200
Chassis & drivetrain
Frame: . . . . Galvanized steel, unit body
Component layout: . . . . Front engine, rear drive
Transmission: . . . . Porsche five-speed all-synchromesh, or four-speed automatic, in unit with differential
Clutch: Through 1986 . . . . Fichtel & Sachs double dry-plate
1987 . . . . Fichtel & Sachs single dry-plate
Rear suspension: . . . . Independent, upper transverse links, lower trailing arms, coil springs, tubular shock absorbers & anti-roll bar
Front suspension: . . . Independent, upper A-arms, lower trailing arms, coil springs, tubular shock absorbers & anti-roll bar
General
Wheelbase, mm/inches: 2500/98.4
Track, front, mm/inches: 1549/61.0
rear, mm/inches: 1521/59.9
Brakes: . . . . . Hydraulic, dual-circuit system, 4 ventilated discs, brake servo, ABS standard
Tire size, front & rear: 225/50VR 16
Wheels: . . . . 7J-16 cast aluminum
Body builder: . . . . Porsche

For 1987 the 928S was given new front and rear end treatment, which improved the looks, and a new designation—928S 4, for the fourth series of development. *Porsche*

Sports car or Grand Touring car? The 928S 4 is both, combining sports car performance with grand touring luxury and refinement. The cost is as dazzling as the car's attributes, but for those who can afford it, the 928S 4 is arguably the best GT car extant. Fast, quiet, comfortable and safe, with ABS braking on four-wheel ventilated disc brakes. *Porsche*

It would seem unlikely that more comfort conveniences can be found to add to the 928, but don't bet against more power and better efficiency in the future. It is indeed a car to take Porsche into the twenty-first century— if the company wants it to do so.

Chapter 12

944

Once again the Frankfurt auto show was the setting for a new Porsche introduction. This time it was September 1981, and the car was the long-awaited 944. I say "long-awaited" advisedly, because the engine had been in the test and development states for at least four years and it seemed almost everyone knew it. And those who didn't, wished for something better than the 924 engine.

This new engine was inevitable for several reasons. Two of the most important being: The 924 engine was a VW/Audi power plant, not even built by Porsche; and the performance of the 924 was anemic at best—certainly not in the Porsche tradition. Porsche management could solve both problems at the same time by creating its own engine. Even though the new engine was installed in a basically standard 924 chassis, this called for a new car designation to make certain everyone knew the car was now an all-Porsche Porsche.

The 944 engine has been called "half a 928" but this is true only to the degree that research, experience and subsequent technology gained from the 928 development have been utilized in the 944 engine. No major part of the 944 engine is interchangeable with a 928. Calling on the experience gained while creating the 928 engine enabled Porsche engineers to design, test and put the 944 four-cylinder into production much faster than they could have done otherwise.

Porsche's parameters for the new engine, aside from requiring performance better than that from the 924, meant that the new engine had to fit into the existing 924 engine compartment (and could be installed from the bottom for production ease) and be as good as possible for both economy and emissions. And by calling on their 928 experience they not only met the goals, but reduced cost and simplified production.

Both cylinder block and head were of Reynolds 390 aluminum alloy, and the crankshaft ran in five main bearings. A single overhead camshaft operated two valves per cylinder through hydraulic tappets, as on the 928, and fuel was fed through a DME (Digital Motor Electronic) fuel injection system which also monitored ignition timing.

Bore and stroke were 100 mm by 78.9 mm, and the total engine displacement was 2479 cc. Compression ratio was 9.5:1 for U.S. models, and 10.6:1 for European delivery cars. Horsepower was 150 DIN (143 SAE) at 5500 rpm for American delivery, and 160 DIN (153 SAE) at 5800 for the European models.

When a four-cylinder engine displaces more than two liters, it can almost be counted on to be a rough-running power plant. Porsche solved this problem by utilizing an idea developed by Frederick W. Lanchester in 1911, and one on which patents are currently held by Mitsubishi. The Lanchester system used two counter-weighted shafts, mounted in the cylinder block, turning twice crankshaft speed (and in the opposite direction to each other), which successfully dampened the vibrations from the large four-cylinder engine.

Drive for these balance shafts as used in the 944 engine came from a toothed Gilmer-type drive belt which had teeth on both sides of the belt—one side driving the right shaft, the other set of teeth driving the left shaft. Porsche engineering had worked on its own balance-shaft design, both to "do it better" and to avoid payment of patent fees. The Porsche men finally came to the conclusion that it would be both expeditious and less costly to use the Mitsubishi design, and pay

the small fee per car—estimated to be around $8.00 each. As one Porsche executive put it: "There's no need to reinvent the motorcar."

In addition to the work done to smooth out the engine, Porsche engineers went to work to cure one of the major complaints against the 924, which was the transmission of vibration and subsequent noise from the 924 engine and drivetrain to the passenger compartment.

At the engine, an anti-freeze-liquid-filled rubber mount (one on each side) was held between a cast-aluminum engine mount and the cast-aluminum frame cross-member. In the middle of the hollow rubber mount was a divider with a small hole, which allowed the fluid to flow back and forth as the engine moved, acting much like a hydraulic shock absorber. At the rear of the car, two more "normal" rubber mounts attached the trans-axle to the unit-body. To further eliminate road-caused vibration through the steering, the steering rack was attached to the chassis by rubber bushings.

Porsche unveiled its new engine, sort of, three months before the Frankfurt show introduction with a "924 GTP (for Grand Touring Prototype) Le Mans" entered in the 1981 running of the twenty-four-hour clas-

The basic body shell and chassis of the 944 were taken directly from the 924 and 924 Turbo, but the flared fenders, to accommodate wider wheels and tires, front air dam and rear-deck spoiler were unique to the 944. Even though introduced to America in May 1982, the 944 was a *1983 model* according to Porsche+Audi—no matter when it was built and sold. *Porsche+Audi*

sic in central France. The car finished third in class and seventh overall. A few weeks later the car ran in a race in Germany.

Outwardly, the car resembled the 924 Carrera, but underneath was a highly-modified 944 engine. During the latter race, the driver pulled into the pits and informed the team manager that his engine was "going." It was running extremely roughly, and seemed down on power. Because it was near the end of the race and they had little to lose, he was told to go back out and finish, which he did. Subsequent dismantling of the engine revealed that one of the balance shafts had slipped a notch on the toothed drive belt—it was worse than having no balance shafts.

Dry weight of the 944 engine was 340 pounds, and dry weight of the car was a bit more than 2,600 pounds, with curb weight at 2,778. All inner body and suspension was that of the 924, but four-wheel ventilated disc brakes from the 924 Turbo were used, and the outer body panels were like those of the 924 Carrera, but made of galvanized steel instead of fiberglass.

Anyone familiar with a 924 interior would feel right at home in the 944. The same seats, instrument panel and other interior accoutrements were as on the 924. A three-spoke, leather-covered steering wheel served the 944 as it had many other Porsche models before, and the wheel still seemed too low to some drivers—there was no height adjustment. New vent outlets were incorporated into the panel on both the 944 and the continuing 924 for European delivery. Sound insulation from the 924 Turbo was carried over as well.

Standard features on the 944 included air conditioning, electrically adjustable outside mirrors, sunroof, power windows, tinted glass, fog lights, 7Jx15 cast alloy wheels, 215/60VR15 steel-belted radial tires and the aforementioned ventilated disc brakes.

Options included a sport suspension package with stiffer shocks, limited-slip differential and 205/55VR16 tires on 7x16 alloy wheels.

Reception of the 944 was the most unanimously enthusiastic ever seen among automotive writers. *AutoWeek, Car and Driver, Motor Trend, Road & Track,* and *VW & Porsche* all wrote about it as if employed by Porsche's advertising agency. And the enthusiasm was not misplaced as far as I can tell. The 944 did everything the 924 should have done, and did it well. It was better looking, it handled better (even though the two chassis were basically the same, the 944 suspension had been tuned just that little bit better) and the factory claimed better acceleration for the 944. Factory figures for the cars are:

924   0–60   10.9 seconds top speed 120
924T 0–60   9.1 seconds top speed 134
944   0–60   8.3 seconds top speed 130

The all-around performance of the 944 was exceptional, and without the complication of the Turbo. At introduction, the 944 was priced at an affordable figure: $18,450. *That* was a bargain price for a Porsche in the year 1982. Even though the 944 was introduced in early 1982, it was, I am told, a 1983 model.

The 944 is too new to judge its impact on automotive history, but it has to rank as one of the better Porsches, by any standard of comparison.

Typically, Porsche engineers have made continual running changes to the 944 and, again, typically, they don't necessarily wait for model or year-end change time. The Digital Motor Electronic (DME) fuel injection was changed to LE-Jetronic (both Bosch), and the welded, stamped-steel front suspension A-arms were replaced by alloy castings, as on the 944 Turbo.

In mid-1985 most of the interior was redone; a smaller steering wheel was mounted just a bit higher, to better clear the driver's legs, and the instruments were regrouped. Top speed for the 143–horsepower car is 130 mph, which is excellent performance considering the power or the price, although the 1987 944 carried a suggested retail price of $25,500—a $7,050 increase over the 1982 introductory price.

At the end of 1985, the 944 Turbo was introduced. Displacement remained the same, the compression ratio was reduced from 9.7:1 to 8.0:1, horsepower went up from 143 to 217 at 5800 rpm, and torque increased from 144 lb-ft at 3000 to 243 at 3500 rpm. Top speed, according to a *Road & Track* test done in late 1985, resulted in 123 mph for a standard 944, and 155 for the 944 Turbo. Elapsed time for the two cars in a quarter-mile acceleration test was 16.6 and 14.6 seconds with top speed at the quarter being 85 and 97.5 mph.

In mid–1986, a yet newer 944, the 944S, came out; this car had a twin-cam, four-valve-per-cylinder head on the same cylinder block. The cylinder head design, like the block, is similar in concept to the 928S, but no parts are interchangeable. A single

Other than the heater control, the 944 interior looks almost identical to the 924 and 924 Turbo. *Greg Brown/Argus*

toothed belt drives the exhaust camshaft which, in turn, drives the intake camshaft via a chain between cylinders two and three.

Horsepower of the 944S is 188 at 6000 rpm, and torque is 170 lb-ft at 4300 rpm. This horsepower gain isn't solely from the adoption of an extra camshaft; the compression ratio is up from 9.7:1 to 10.9:1, and both intake and exhaust ports (and manifold runners) are larger.

Claimed top speed for the 944S is 228 km/h (142 mph) which is not only reasonable, but probably conservative. I've driven a 944S at 255 km/h on the autobahn, which translates to 158 mph. Assuming a ten percent speedometer error, which I doubt, that comes out almost exactly 142 mph. To cope with this performance, both the 944S and 944 Turbo have ABS four-channel braking systems optional for 1987. Porsche tests indicated that a 944 with ABS will stop in eighty to eighty-seven percent of the distance required for a non-ABS-equipped car at 100 km/h (62 mph), and approximately eighty-five to ninety-five percent of the distance from 150 km/h (93 mph)—the higher numbers being for dry road conditions and

Standard equipment on the 944S included air conditioning, electric window, outside mirrors, fog lights and the sunroof. *Porsche+Audi*

the lower, better numbers for slippery roads.

And, if that fails to save the errant driver from his or her own stupidity (a driver would have to be stupid to get a 944S in serious trouble), airbags, for both driver and passenger, are standard on the 944 Turbo, and optional on the 944 and 944S. Porsche thus became the first car company to offer airbags for passengers as well as drivers.

All Porsche 944 models—944, 944S, 944 Turbo, and 944 Turbo S—retained the 2479 cc, inline, water-cooled four-cylinder engine for 1988. All but the 944S, which has a twin overhead camshaft, sixteen-valve cylinder head, have the now familiar sohc eight-valve head.

Horsepower ratings are 158 for the 944, 188 for the 944S, 217 for the Turbo, and 247 for the Turbo S. The three carryover models had little change, but the list of standard equipment gets bigger each year. Standard equipment for 1988 included air conditioning, power windows and steering, central locking, rear spoiler, electric height adjustment for the driver's seat, heated rear window, and brake pad wear indicator.

The 944S and Turbo contain those standard features plus airbags for driver and passenger. The Turbo also comes with partial leather seats, four-piston fixed-caliper

The twin-cam, four-valve-per-cylinder-head 944S was introduced in mid–1986. It produced 190 DIN or 188 SAE horsepower at 6000 rpm. In 1989, displacement was raised from 2.5 to 3.0 liters and horsepower was increased to 208 SAE at 5800 rpm, and the designation changed to 944 S2. *Porsche*

A distinctive front-end treatment marks the 944 Turbo difference from other 944 models. The "bowling ball" wheels are similar to the ones for the 928. The Turbo should top 150 mph in fifth, and do 0–60 in six seconds, the quarter mile in 14.6, with 97.5 mph at the end of the quarter. *Porsche*

ventilated disc brakes, and pressure-cast alloy wheels.

A new model, introduced in February to be built in a run of 700 cars, was the 944 Turbo S. With thirty more horsepower (247 to 217) than the Turbo, 0–60 mph comes up in 5.5 seconds and top speed is rated at 162 miles per hour. To accommodate the added performance, the Turbo S has firmer springs and shock absorbers, larger anti-roll bars, and more rigid suspension bushings.

Forged alloy wheels—seven inches wide in front, nine inches at the rear—are fitted with 225/50 VR 16 front tires and 245/45 VR 16 rear tires. All standard equipment for the other 944 models is included in the 944 Turbo S specifications.

For 1989, the 944 line was reduced to three models—944, 944 S2, and 944 Turbo—but for the first time a cabriolet became an option as the 944 S2 Cabriolet.

The price leader, at least for Porsches, was the 944 coupe at $36,360, but it offered a lot more than before. A bore increase of 4 mm, to 104, increased displacement to 2682 cc and that, along with a higher compression ratio (up to 10.9:1 from 10.6) raised horsepower to 162 at 5800 rpm. Anti-lock brakes were also made standard on all 944 models.

Other standard equipment included all that listed for 1988, plus electric tilt removable sunroof, heated rear window, cruise control, and a one-key central locking and alarm system with LED in the door lock buttons to show when the alarm is engaged.

For 1990 the 944 series was whittled down to two cars, the 944 S2 Coupe and Cabriolet, with a 208 hp, 3.0-liter engine. The 2.7-liter 162 hp 944 Coupe, and the 2.5-liter, 247 hp Turbo are no longer available. Anti-lock braking, and both driver and passenger side airbag restraints are standard on all 1990 Porsches.

The reduction of models and variations, with a definite move toward the higher priced end of the market, was deliberate on Porsche's part to put more emphasis on the company's high-tech and upscale market position. Porsche no longer believes that the company can profitably produce any car that would be considered entry level or near entry level.

---

944 (1982–89) & 944T (1986–89)

Engine
Design: .... Water-cooled inline four
Borexstroke, mm/inches (1982–1988): 100x78.9/3.94x3.11
  (1989): 103.8x78.9/4.09x3.11
Displacement, cc/cubic inches (1982–1988): 2479/151
  (1989): 2688/164
Valve operation: .... Toothed belt-driven single overhead camshaft
Compression ratio, Europe & Great Britain
  (1982–1988): 10.6:1
  U.S., Canada, Japan (1982–1988): 9.5:1
  (1989): 10.9:1
  944T (1986–1989): 8.0:1
Carburetion 944: .... Electronic fuel injection with oxygen sensor DME controlled
  944T: .... Same, with KKK turbocharger
BHP (Mfr) 944 (1982–1985): .... 150 DIN/143 SAE @ 5800
  (1986–1989): .... 147 SAE @ 5800
  944T (1986–1988): .... 217 SAE @ 5800
  (1988 & 1989 Turbo S*): .... 247 SAE @ 6000

Chassis & drivetrain
Frame: .... Unit-body
Component layout: .... Front engine, rear drive
Clutch: .... Fichtel & Sachs single dry-plate
Transmission: .... Porsche five-speed all-synchromesh, in unit with differential; optional three-speed automatic, in-unit with differential
Axle ratio: with five-speed 3.89:1
  with three-speed automatic 3.45:1
Rear suspension: ...... Independent, semi-trailing arms, transverse torsion bars & tubular shock absorbers (rear anti-roll bar optional)
Front suspension: .... Independent, MacPherson telescopic shock strut & lower A-arm on each side with coil springs & anti-roll bar

General
Wheelbase, mm/inches: 2400/94.5
Track, front, mm/inches: 1478/58.2
  rear, mm/inches: 1450/57.1
Brakes: .... Disc
Tire size, front & rear: .... 215/60VR 15 (205/55VR 16 with optional wheels)
Wheels: .... 7Jx15 cast alloy (7Jx16 forged alloy optional)
Body builder: .... Porsche
*470 944S Turbos were built in 1988 as a special edition.

The 944 interior (944S shown) is unique to the model, but the instrument layout is similar to the 911 series. Driver and passenger comfort are much better than the 924 series cars, primarily because of steering wheel placement. The 944 can reasonably claim to be the best new Porsche for the dollar. *Porsche*

A Cabriolet 944 S2 was first offered in 1989 (top). The Cabrio body was not available on the 944 or 944 Turbo and for 1990 the S2 Coupe and S2 Cabriolet (bottom) were the only 944 models available. *Porsche*

944S (1986–88) & 944 S2 (1989–)

Engine
Design: . . . . Water-cooled inline four
Borexstroke, mm/inches (1986–1988): 100x78.9/3.94/3.11
(S2 1989–): 103.8x87.9/4.09/3.46
Displacement, cc/cubic inches (1986–1988): 2479/151
(S2 1989–): 2990/183
Valve operation: . . . . Toothed belt-driven twin overhead
camshafts, four valves per cylinder
Compression ratio: 10.9:1
Carburetion: . . . . Bosch Motronic M2.1 fuel injection
BHP (Mfr) 944S: . . . . 188 @ 6000
944 S2: . . . . 208 @ 5800

Chassis & drivetrain
Frame: . . . . Unit body
Component layout: . . . . Front engine, rear drive
Clutch: . . . . Fichtel & Sachs single dry-plate
with diaphragm spring, hydraulic operation
Transmission: . . . . Porsche five-speed all-
synchromesh, in unit with differential

Axle ratio: 3.889:1
Rear suspension: . . . . Independent, semi-
trailing arms, transverse torsion bars &
tubular shock absorbers, anti-roll bar
Front suspension: . . . . Independent,
MacPherson telescopic shock strut & lower
A-arm on each side with coil springs & anti-roll bar

General
Wheelbase, mm/inches: 2400/94.5
Track, front, mm/inches: 1477/58.1
rear, mm/inches: 1451/57.1
Brakes: . . . . . Hydraulic, dual-circuit system, 4 ventilated discs,
brake servo, optional ABS (ABS standard 1989 on)
Tire size, front & rear: (standard) . . . . 195/65 VR 15
(optional) . . . . 205/55 VR 16–225/50 VR 16
Wheels, front and rear: (standard) . . . . 7J-16 cast aluminum
(optional) . . . . 7J-16–8J-16 forged aluminum
Body builder: . . . . Porsche

149

The rare and exotic

★ ★ ★ ★ ★

A rare piece is this Glockler Spyder which is a "homebuilt" using Porsche parts. Max Hoffman brought the car to America, raced it briefly, and sold it, to be raced by Karl Brocken and Ed Trego. The Glockler Spyders were the predecessors of the Porsche 550 Spyders. *Author*

★ ★ ★ ★ ★

Two pushrod Spyders originally built for Le Mans ran in the Carrera Panamericana in 1953.

Fernando Segura drove No. 154 to second in class and thirty-third overall. These were Spyders with coupe tops added. *Author*

★ ★ ★ ★ ★
Early 550 Spyders, circa 1953, still had pushrod
engines. This is Johnny von Neumann at Pebble
Beach in 1954, in one of the first Spyders seen in
the United States. *Ralph Poole*

★ ★ ★ ★ ★
The late Ken Miles in von Neumann's 550A. This
one with the four-cam engine. The basic body
configuration is similar to the pushrod Spyders,
but has a lower rear fender profile, only two
louvers on the rear fender flanks. The two
scoops in the front of the body for brake cooling
were added later. *Ralph Poole*

★ ★ ★ ★ ★
Front of a 550A/1500RS "customer" Spyder.
This model retained the ladder-type frame of
the 550 Spyder while the factory 550A/1500RS
had a small-diameter tube space frame. *Ralph
Poole*

★ ★ ★ ★ ★
When the 550A/1500RS came out, it had
smoother front fender/light treatment; sometimes fairings covered the headlights as on Jack
McAfee's 88. The factory cars had tubular space
frames, the customer 550A still had the tubular
ladder-type frame of the 550 Spyder. *Ralph
Poole*

★ ★ ★ ★ ★

The model 718, known as the RSK, was introduced in mid–1957 as the successor to the 550A/1500RS. The RSK utilized the same space frame, and the wheelbase and track were the same as the 1500RS, but the body was thinner, reducing aerodynamic drag somewhat. In 1958, some RSKs had small fins on the rear fenders, and a center-seater was built for Jean Behra to race at Reims as a Formula 2 car. In the top photo the foreground car is a standard RSK while the car behind it is a new "RSK" body built on a 911 chassis by Jack Hagemann. *Author*

★ ★ ★ ★ ★
Porsche RS 60 was built to conform to FIA rules requiring not only legal road equipment, but other amenities as well; windshield, top and luggage accommodation. There is no record of an RS 60 competing with top up or suitcase in place. *Kurt Worner/Road & Track*

★ ★ ★ ★ ★

One of the most sought-after, and coveted Porsches is the Abarth Carrera; indecently fast and brutally handsome, but not altogether practical for daily commuting or Sunday drives in the country. Less than 20 were made, starting out as 1600s in 1960/61 and some were retrofitted to 2-liter engines later. The only thing more impressive than the look of the Carrera engine is the sound from all those gears, shafts, cams and roller bearings when it starts up. The sound from the exhaust of a Carrera in full flight is not soon forgotten. *Author and Greg Brown/Argus*

★ ★ ★ ★ ★
Herbert Linge and Edgar Barth shared the wheel of this 2000GS–GT to finish third overall in the 1963 Targa Florio. It was on a 356B chassis with Carrera 2 engine. Only two were built. *Author*

★ ★ ★ ★
Karozzerie Beutler, in Thun, Switzerland, produced several bodies for Porsche running gear. This is a four-passenger coupe based on the 1962 356B. Bumpers, lights, door handles, wheels and hubcaps appear to be stock items. The wheelbase also appears to be unchanged from the stock 82.7 inches. *Road & Track*

★ ★ ★ ★ ★

The 904 GTS is considered the ultimate factory racer by some, and the ultimate road machine by others. The "others" probably haven't driven one on the road. Without severe reworking, it is almost impossible to carry a passenger as the second seat is there to satisfy the FIA rules, not to accommodate a passenger in comfort. The 904 frame is a boxed section assembly with the fiberglass body bonded to it, and it's the one four-cylinder, four-cam Carrera with no chassis or body ties to the 356 line. *Leonard Turner*

★ ★ ★ ★ ★

Another "plastic Porsche," the 906 Carrera 6. A few of these get driven on the street occasionally but they were built as race cars and their primary function is to go fast. More of them are turning up at historic car races, Porsche club competition events and even concours. *Leonard Turner*

★ ★ ★ ★

In 1967, the Troutman-Barnes shop, then in Culver City, California, converted a 911S into a four-door sedan for William J. Dick, Jr., co-owner of Porsche Cars Southwest in San Antonio, Texas. The result was a Christmas present for Mrs. Dick. Four matching leather-upholstered seats were made by Porsche in Stuttgart, and extra hides were sent to Troutman-Barnes which had Tony Nancy do the rest of the interior trim to match the seats. A final touch was the installation of electric window lifts, and a Sportomatic transmission. *Ralph Poole*

★ ★ ★ ★ ★

Conceived in 1971 as a 1972 model, the 916 was going to be Porsche's answer to the Ferrari Dino V-6. Visually the 916 looked like the 914/6 GT, but the top was permanently attached to the body for extra stiffness. Fuchs five-spoke alloy wheels with seven-inch rims carried 185/70-15 Michelin tires. Spacers (21 mm in front, 27 mm at the rear) increased the track width about two inches over the 914. Ventilated disc brakes were used on all four wheels, Bilstein competition shock absorbers were standard as was an anti-roll bar at each end. The 916 engine was taken from the 1972 911S, and in its fuel-injected form it produced 190 DIN horsepower at 6500 rpm. Because it weighed less than the 911S by 165 pounds, the 916 was the fastest accelerating Porsche for 1972. The five-speed transmission shift was arranged with the lower four gears in the traditional H pattern with fifth up and to the right. The unique interior of the 916 was rather gaudy for a Porsche of that period and featured leather trim on seats and door panels with velour seat inserts—all color-keyed to the instrument panel and carpet. After the first 20 cars were built the decision was made to not proceed with the model. Instruments consisted of a tach in the center of the panel, a speedometer at the right and a combined oil temperature and pressure gauge (as on the 911) at the left. A small fuel gauge was mounted under the dash on the console. *Porsche+Audi*

★ ★ ★ ★ ★
A 924 Turbo outfitted to run at Le Mans in 1980,
and as a car to replace the 930 Turbo as a private
entrant racing car. *Porsche+Audi*

★ ★ ★ ★ ★

For many years, single-seat racing cars—Grand Prix, F-2, Indianapolis, etc—were a drug on the market because there was no place to use them. Starting about 1986, vintage car racing embraced the open-wheeled cars and their value has skyrocketed. This is the 1962 Porsche Type 804 Grand Prix car. Its flat eight, 1494 cc engine put out 180 hp. Dan Gurney won the 1962 French Grand Prix at Rouen, France, in one of these. *Leonard Turner*

★ ★ ★ ★ ★

One of Porsche's greatest racing cars, the 917K, as raced by John Wyer in the early 1970s. The normally-aspirated flat 12, dohc 4.9–liter engine produced 600 horsepower at 8400 rpm. These are not cars for the dilettante driver as superb skill and great bravery are required to extract anything like maximum performance from them. *Leonard Turner*

★ ★ ★ ★ ★

The first Porsche open-wheel single seater was this four-cylinder, four-cam-powered car that ran in Formula 2 but was later eligible for Formula 1 when F1 engine limits were lowered to 1500 cc. Not as fast as the 804 eight cylinder, it was nevertheless a reliable finisher and often achieved good finished running against faster but less reliable cars. *Porsche Panorama*

Numbering system

The Porsche design department assigned numbers, in sequence, for all projects going through the company. Following is a list of the numbers relating directly to Porsche cars (dated either by starting or introduction of the car design), plus a few of the more interesting non-Porsche car projects. The list is not complete, partly because of the Porsche company's secrecy about its clients, or because of a number's irrelevance to Porsche cars.

Number	Year	Description
7	1930	Wanderer car chassis design
22	1932–37	Auto Union Grand Prix car
52	1934	Auto Union sports car
60	1934–41	KdF car (to become the Volkswagen)
60K10	1939	KdF sports coupe for Berlin-Rome race
64	1937–38	KdF sports car
80	1938–39	Mercedes-Benz land speed record car
82	1939–40	KdF-based military Kubelwagen
87	1939–41	4-wheel-drive Kubelwagen
108	1938	2-stage supercharger for Mercedes-Benz
114	1938–39	F-wagen, 1.5-liter Porsche sports car
128	1940–41	KdF-based amphibian Schwimmwagen
205	1942	180-ton tank Maus
212	1942	16-cylinder, air-cooled diesel tank engine
245	1942	18-ton multipurpose tank
309	1945	2-stroke diesel engine

Number	Year	Description
323	1946	11-hp diesel tractor
356	1947	First production Porsche, VW-based
356/2	1947–48	Gmünd-built Porsche sports car
356A	1955–58	Production Porsche
356B	1959–62	Production Porsche, T–5 body
356C	1963–64	Production Porsche, T–6 body
360	1947–48	Cisitalia 4-wheel-drive GP car
369	1949–50	1.1-liter engine for 356 and 356/2
370	1947	Cisitalia 1.5-liter sports/touring car
502	1950–51	1.5-liter engine for 356
506	1950–51	1.3-liter engine for 356
506/2	1954–55	Type 506 with 3-piece crankcase
514	1951	1951 Le Mans cars (356SL)
519	1951–52	Synchromesh transmission for 356
522	1952	Strut-type front suspension proposal for VW
527	1951–52	60-hp, 1.5-liter engine for 356
528	1952–53	1500S, or Super, engine for 356
530	1951–52	Experimental 4-passenger Porsche
540	1952	America roadster & Speedster bodies
546	1952–53	Plain-bearing version of 527 (1500, or Normal)
546/2	1954–55	Type 546 with 3-piece crankcase
547	1952–53	Four camshaft, 1.5-liter racing engine
547/1	1955	Series-built Type 547 (1.5-liter)

Number	Year	Description
547/3	1958	Improved 1.5-liter engine for 718 & 718/2
547/4	1957	1.6-liter engine for 718
547/5	1957	1.7-liter engine for 718
550	1953	Mid-engine, 2-seat sports/racing car
550A/1500RS	1956	Redesigned 550 with tubular space frame
587	1961	2.0-liter engine for 718
587/1	1961–62	Touring version of 587 for Carrera 2
587/2	1963	Racing version of 587/1
587/3	1963–64	Improved 2.0-liter engine for 904
589	1953–54	1.3-liter engine for 1300S
589/2	1954–55	Type 589 with 3-piece crankcase
597	1954–55	Jagdwagen (Hunter) 4-wheel-drive vehicle
616/1	1955–56	1.6-liter engine for 356A 1600
616/2	1955–56	1.6-liter engine for 356A 1600S
616/3	1956	1.6-liter industrial engine
616/7	1960	1.6-liter S–90 engine for 356B
616/12	1961–62	Type 616/2 with cast-iron cylinders
616/15	1963–64	1.6-liter engine for 356C
616/16	1963–64	1.6-liter engine for 356SC
616/36	1965	1.6-liter engine for 912
616/39	1967–68	616/36 with U.S. emission control
644	1957	4-speed transmission for 356B
645	1956	Sports racing car "Mickey Mouse"
678	1959	1.6-liter engine (aircraft)
690	1958	5-speed tunnel-case transmission for 718
692	1958	Improved 4-camshaft Carrera engine
692/0	1958	1.5-liter 692 (roller bearing crankshaft)
692/1	1958	1.5-liter 692 (plain-bearing crankshaft)
692/2	1958	1.6-liter Type 692 for touring Carrera
695	1959	Porsche disc brake
718	1957	Sports racing car (RSK)
718/2	1959	1.5-liter single-seat racing car (F–2)
729	1958	Marine engine
745	1962	Experimental 2.0- and 2.2-liter six-cylinder engines
753	1961–62	1.5-liter 8-cylinder for Type 804 GP car
771	1962	2.0- and 2.2-liter versions of 753
787	1961	Grand Prix car chassis
804	1962	Grand Prix car chassis
901	1963	Prototype 6-cylinder sports car
901/0	1964–65	5-speed transmission for 901/911
901/01	1964–65	130-hp engine for 901/911
901/02	1966–67	160-hp engine, 5-speed transmission for 911S
901/03	1967–68	110 horsepower engine, 5-speed transmission for 911T
901/05	1966	901/01 with Weber carburetors
901/06	1966–67	901/05 with revised valve timing
901/07	1967–68	901/06 for Sportomatic
901/08	1967–68	901/02 for Sportomatic
901/09	1968–69	911E fuel-injected engine
901/10	1968–69	911S fuel-injected engine, 4-speed transmission
901/13	1967–68	901/3 for Sportomatic
901/14	1967–68	901/06 with U.S. emission control
901/17	1967–68	901/14 for Sportomatic
901/20	1966	210-hp engine for 906, Carrera 6
901/21	1966–67	Fuel injected 901/20 for 906E, 910/6
901/22	1967	210-hp engine for 911R
901/30	1968	150-hp rally kit for 911L
902/0	1965–66	4-speed transmission for 911, 912
902/01	1967–68	4-speed transmission for 912
902/02	1967–68	5-speed transmission for 912
902/1	1965–66	5-speed transmission for 911, 912
904	1963–64	Mid-engined competition GT coupe (904 GTS)
904/6	1964	(Unofficial) 904 with 6-cylinder engine
904/8	1964	(Unofficial) 904 with 8-cylinder engine
905/00	1967–68	4-speed Sportomatic transmission
905/13	1968–69	4-speed Sportomatic transmission
906	1966	Competition sports coupe (space frame)
906/8	1966	(Unofficial) 906 with 8-cylinder engine
906E	1966–67	906 with fuel injection, modified body
907	1968	Sports racing coupe, short tail, right-hand drive
907L	1967–68	907 with long tail
908	1968	3.0-liter, 8-cylinder engine and car

Number	Year	Description	Number	Year	Description
908/01	1969	908 with coupe body	911/73	1972	2466 cc racing engine for 911S
908/02	1969	908 with open body (spyder)	911/74	1973	3.0-liter racing engine for Carrera RSR
908/03	1970	908 with open body (spyder)	911/75	1973	911/74 with slide throttle
908K	1968	908 with short-tail coupe body	911/76	1974	2.1 Turbo engine for RSR
908L	1968	908 with long-tail coupe body	911/77	1973–74	3.0-liter engine for Carrera RS
909	1968	2.0-liter hill climb spyder	911/81	1975–76	2.7-liter engine for 911
910	1966–67	Sports racing coupe	911/82	1975–76	2.7-liter engine for 49-state 911S
910/6	1967	910 with 2.0-liter 6-cylinder engine (901/21)	911/83	1972–73	2.7-liter engine for Carrera RS
910/8	1967	910 with 2.2-liter 8-cylinder engine (771)	911/84	1975–76	2.7-liter engine for California 911S
910/8B	1967–68	910/8, lightened for hillclimbs	911/86	1975–76	911/81 for Sportomatic
911	1964–65	6-cylinder production model (from 901)	911/89	1975–76	2.7-liter engine for Sportomatic (U.S.)
911/00	1969–70	4-speed transmission for 911T	911/91	1973	2.4-liter CIS injection engine for 911T (U.S.)
911/01	1969–70	2.2-liter engine for 911E	911/92	1973–74	2.7-liter for 911
911/02	1969–70	2.2-liter 180 horsepower engine for 911S	911/93	1973–74	2.7-liter engine for 911S and U.S. Carrera
911/04	1969–70	911/01 engine for Sportomatic	911/96	1973	911/91 for Sportomatic
911/06	1969–70	911/03 engine for Sportomatic	911/97	1973–74	911/92 for Sportomatic
911/07	1969–70	2.2-liter engine for 911T	911/98	1973–74	911/93 for Sportomatic
911/08	1969–70	911/07 engine for Sportomatic	911E	1968–69	Fuel-injected model between 911T and 911S
911/20	1970	2247 cc engine for competition 911S	911L	1967–68	Top-line model for U.S., intermediate model for Europe
911/21	1971	2381 cc engine for competition 911S	911R	1967	911S lightweight racing model
911/22	1970	911/20 with carburetors instead of fuel injection	911S	1966–67	High-performance touring model of 911
911/41	1974–75	2.7-liter engine for 911	911T	1967–68	911 model tuned for all-around road performance
911/42	1974–75	2.7-liter engine for 911S			
911/43	1974–75	2.7-liter engine for 49-state 911	912	1965	4-cylinder version of 911
911/44	1974–75	2.7-liter engine for California 911	912	1969	4.5-liter, 12-cylinder racing engine for 917
911/46	1974–75	911/41 for Sportomatic	912E	1975–76	Fuel-injected 4-cylinder engine/car
911/47	1974–75	911/42 for Sportomatic	914	1969–70	4-cylinder, mid-engined car
911/48	1974–75	911/43 for Sportomatic	914/6	1969–70	6-cylinder version of 914
911/49	1974–75	911/44 for Sportomatic	914/8	1969	914/6 with 908 3-liter engine
911/51	1971–72	2.4-liter engine for American 911T	914/11	1969–70	5-speed transmission for 914 and 914/6
911/52	1971–72	2.4-liter engine for 911E	914/12	1972–73	5-speed transmission for 914
911/53	1971–72	2.4-liter engine for 911S	915	1971–72	Stronger 4- or 5-speed transmission for 911
911/57	1971–72	2.4-liter engine for European 911T	915/06	1973–74	5-speed transmission for 911, 911S, Carrera
911/61	1971–72	911/51 for Sportomatic	915/08	1972–73	5-speed transmission for Carrera RS
911/62	1971–72	911/52 for Sportomatic			
911/63	1971–72	911/53 for Sportomatic			
911/67	1971–72	911/57 for Sportomatic			
911/70	1971	2494 cc racing engine for 911S			
911/72	1972–73	2.8-liter racing engine for 911S, Carrera RSR			

Number	Year	Description	Number	Year	Description
915/12	1971–72	4-speed transmission for 911T, 911E, 911S	917K	1969–70	Short-tail version of 917
915/16	1973–74	4-speed transmission for 911, 911S, Carrera	917L	1970	Long-tail version of 917 (Le Mans)
915/40	1974–75	5-speed transmission for 911S, U.S. Carrera	917PA	1969	917 Spyder (Can Am)
			923	1975–76	2.0-liter engine for 912E
915/43	1974–75	5-speed transmission for 911	924	1976–77	Water-cooled, front-engined production car
915/44	1975–76	5-speed transmission for 911, U.S. 911S	925/00	1971–72	4-speed Sportomatic for 911T, 911E
915/45	1974–75	4-speed transmission for 911S	925/01	1971–72	4-speed Sportomatic for 911S
915/48	1974–75	4-speed transmission for 911	925/02	1973–74	4-speed Sportomatic for 911, 911S, U.S. Carrera
915/49	1975–76	4-speed transmission for 911	925/09	1975–76	3-speed Sportomatic for 911
916	1967	DOHC racing engine version of 901	925/10	1974–75	3-speed Sportomatic for 911S, Carrera (U.S.)
916	1968	5-speed transmission for 908/01, 908/02	925/12	1975–76	3-speed Sportomatic for 911, U.S. 911S
916	1971	Projected 2.4-liter version of 914/6	928	1977–78	Water-cooled, front V-8-engined production car
917	1969	4.5-liter, 12-cylinder sports racing coupe	930	1974–75	911-based Turbo and Turbo Carrera
917/10	1971–72	4.5-liter, 12-cylinder sports racing spyder (Can Am)	930/10	1974–75	Turbocharged engine for 930
917/20	1971	917K, low-drag coupe body	934	1975–76	Group 4 racing 930 Turbo coupe
			935	1976	Group 5 racing 930 Turbo coupe
917/30	1973	Further development of 917/10 (Can Am)	936	1976	Group 6 turbocharged spyder

Parts and service sources

California
American International Racing
149 E. Santa Anita
Burbank, CA 91502
Special body panels, accessories

NPR of America, Inc.
7625 E. Rosecrans Ave. #33
Paramount, CA 90723
Big-bore cylinder kits for 914

Mitcom
12621 Sherman Way
North Hollywood, CA 91605
Fiberglass body panels

Ansen
13217 E. Rosecrans Ave.
Santa Fe Springs, CA 90670
Alloy wheels

The Parts Shop
15571 Producer Lane, Unit J
Huntington Beach, CA 92649
Mechanical & rubber parts

Prestige Motoring Accessories
18195 Euclid St.
Fountain Valley, CA 92708
Accessories, car covers

Aase Brothers, Inc.
701 E. Cypress
Anaheim, CA 92805
New & used Porsche parts

Traction Master Co.
2917 W. Olympic Blvd.
Los Angeles, CA 90006
Boge shock absorbers

W-W Wheel Adapters
9103-6 E. Garvey Ave.
Rosemead, CA 91770
4-lug to 5-lug wheel adapters

Gene Berg Enterprises
1725 N. Lime St.
Orange, CA 92665
Porsche industrial engines

Porsche Graphics
14737 Calvert St.
Van Nuys, CA 91401
Porsche color lithographs

Competition Engineering
2095 N. Lake Ave.
Altadena, CA 91001
High-performance engine parts

Garretson Enterprises
1932 Old Middlefield Way
Mt. View, CA 94043
Service, parts, accessories

Rennsport Werke
320 Martin Ave.
Santa Clara, CA 95050
4-cam, 4-cylinder repair & service

Enex Corporation
P.O. Box 66515
Los Angeles, CA 90066
Restoration, fabrication, machining

Martin Schneider Design Systems
9063 W. Washington Blvd.
Culver City, CA 90230
Headers, turbochargers

Design Dimensions
33 Montecito Drive
Corte Madera, CA 94925
Porsche coveralls

Dial-A-Cam
19361 Lake Chabot Road
Castro Valley, CA 94546
Performance camshafts

Bob Bondurant
Sears Point Int'l. Raceway
Sonoma, CA 95476
Racing & survival-driving
instruction

Parts & Polish
12952 W. Washington Blvd.
Los Angeles, CA 90066
Performance parts, accessories

International Racing Services, Inc.
13332 W. Washington Blvd.
Los Angeles, CA 90066
Catalytic & thermal reactor
replacements

Eurometrix
P.O. Box 1361
Campbell, CA 95008
Weber & Solex carburetor rebuild

Claude's Buggies, Inc.
28813 Farmersville Blvd.
Farmersville, CA 93223
Weber carburetors, manifolds,
ignitions

International Mercantile
P.O. Box 3178
Long Beach, CA 90803
Obsolete rubber & trim

Robert W. Wood, Inc.
1340 Club View Drive
Los Angeles, CA 90024
Wheels, new & refinished

PB Tweeks West
4001 E. Anaheim
Long Beach, CA 90804
Body & engine parts, accessories

Autos International
148 N. Cedros
Solana Beach, CA 92075
Carpets, headliners, tops

House of Porsche
233 Weddell Drive
Sunnyvale, CA 94086
Restoration, race preparation

Troutman
3198L Airport Loop Drive
Costa Mesa, CA 92626
Body parts for 911, 914, 924 & 930

PC Ltd.
P.O. Box 733
Simi Valley, CA 93062
Porsche parts & accessories

Alan Johnson Racing
5220 Gaines St.
San Diego, CA 92110
Racing preparation & parts

Porsche Mailorder
135 17th St.
Santa Monica, CA 90402
Weber carburetors & manifolds

Automotion
3535 W. Kifer Road
Santa Clara, CA 95051
Parts, accessories, books

BAE
3032 Kashiwa St.
Torrance, CA 90505
Turbochargers

Porsche Parts Obsolete
2950 Randolph
Costa Mesa, CA 92626
NOS & used Porsche parts

Boge of America
17965 Sky Park Blvd. #A
Irvine, CA 92714
Boge shock absorbers

H. G. Bieker Co.
918 Chestnut St.
Burbank, CA 91506
Machining, repairs, rebuilding

Performance Products
16129 Leadwell
Van Nuys, CA 91406
914 stainless rocker panels

Johnny's Speed and Chrome
6411 Beach Blvd.
Buena Park, CA 90621
Parts, accessories

KM Products
P.O. Box 43
Tujunga, CA 91402
924 rear lens conversion

Far Horizon Auto Accessories
1905 E. Deere Ave.
Santa Ana, CA 92705
Accessories, parts

Highland Plating Co.
1128 N. Highland Ave.
Los Angeles, CA 90038
Plating & polishing

American Eagle Wheel Corp.
15622 Chemical Lane
Huntington Beach, CA 92649
Alloy wheels

Pro Parts
4113 Redwood Ave.
Los Angeles, CA 90066
Car covers, exhausts, clothing

Valleycore
10057 Mills Station Rd. Box 26004
Sacramento, CA 95827
Engine parts

Y n Z's Yesterday's Parts
1615 W. Fern Ave.
Redlands, CA 92373
356 wiring harnesses

Autoscarrera
P.O. Box 6223
San Diego, CA 92106
Repro Speedster seats

Erickson Engine Service
P.O. Box 5323
Long Beach, CA 90805
Chain tensioners

IFI Products
25381-G Alicia Parkway, Suite 306
Laguna Hills, CA 93653
911 rear speaker replacements

Vintage Porsche
P.O. Box 7095
Long Beach, CA 90807
Appraisal, restoration, history

Continental Foreign Auto Parts
12525 Sherman Way
North Hollywood, CA 91605
Used Porsche parts

Creative Arts Unlimited
P.O. Box 1824
Fremont, CA 94583
Porsche pins

TFA Car Co.
11568 Sorrento Valley Rd. Suite 9
San Diego, CA 92121
Porsche soft pillows

Bill Yates Racing Service
32852 Valle Rd.
San Juan Capistrano, CA 92675
Competition engine parts

Auto Racing Posters
1360 Gladys Ave.
Long Beach, CA 90804
German decals, posters, catalogs

Porsche Aire
9519 East Artesia Blvd.
Bellflower, CA 90706
Porsche air conditioning

Colorado
Lawrence A. Braun
329 East First St.
Loveland, CO 80537
Bronze sculptures

HRH Enterprises
P.O. Box 6833
Denver, CO 80206
Belt buckles

Art-on-Wheels
2029 Eagle View Dr.
Colorado Springs, CO 80909
Desk name plaques

Toad Hall Motorbooks
1235 Pierce St.
Lakewood, CO 80214
Porsche books

Connecticut
Callaway Turbo Systems
Stewarts Corner
Lyme, CT 06371
Turbocharger systems

Florida
Meldeau Tire World
2270 N. Semoran Blvd.
Winter Park, FL 32792
Tires, wheels

Porsche Plus
12109 Landing Blvd.
Cooper City, FL 33026
Parts, accessories

Triad Industries, Inc.
P.O. Box 142
Sarasota, FL 33578
Exhaust systems, heat exchangers

Webb's Machine Design
2251 Sunset Point Road
Clearwater, FL 33515
911 stainless steel airbox

Graku Competition Wheels, Inc.
P.O. Box 350186
Fort Lauderdale, FL 33316
Alloy wheels

Dean's Wheels and Accessories
6264 Arthur Durham Drive
Jacksonville, FL 32210
Alloy wheels

Porsche VW Auto Works
107 Longwood Ave.
Altamonte Springs, FL 32701
Restoration, paint, bodywork

Turboglas
3402 N.E. 2nd St.
Gainesville, FL 32601
Fiberglass custom body parts

Florida VW & Porsche
P.O. Box 4492
Hialeah, FL 33014
Parts, accessories

Group 5
3140 Pembroke Rd.
Hallandale, FL 33009
Parts, accessories

Classic Motor Carriages, Inc.
16650 NW 27th Ave.
Miami, FL 33054
356 Speedster replicar kit

Addco
96F Watertower Rd.
Lake Park, FL 33403
Anti-roll bars

S.S. Inc.
1665 Lexington Ave. Suite 105C
DeLand, FL 32720
Porsche designer jeans

Georgia
PB Tweeks South
6483 Peachtree Industrial Blvd.
Atlanta, GA 30040
Body & engine parts,
accessories

Automobile Atlanta
504 Clay St.
Marietta, GA 30060
914 parts

Avril Exclusive Ltd.
200 W. Wieuca Rd.
Atlanta, GA 30342
Speepskin seat covers, gloves

Turbo Oil & Gas
188 Barrett Industrial Way
Norcross, GA 30017
Alloy wheel cleaners

FAF Imports
3862 Stephens Ct.
Tucker, GA 30084
Accessories, shock absorbers

Porsche Atlanta
8 Steve Drive
Doraville, GA 30340
Porsche parts

CB&E
899 Burns Dr.
Marietta, GA 30067
356 & 911 interior resto kits

Illinois
Williams Motorcar Services
213 Westbrook Dr.
Springfield, IL 62702
356 & 911 luggage tie-downs

Indiana
PB Tweeks, Ltd.
4410 N. Keystone
Indianapolis, IN 46205
Body & engine parts,
accessories

Initial Concepts
P.O. Box 3629
South Bend, IN 46619
Accessories

Kentucky
Louisville Lock & Key, Inc.
317 Wallace Center #204D
Louisville, KY 40207
Anti-theft devices

Louisiana
Human Accessories
1025 Olive St.
Shreveport, LA 71101
Porsche sweaters

Maine
Pine Hill Automotive
Pine Hill Road
Berwick, ME 03901
Rubber seals, trim pieces

Massachusetts
Speedmark Limited
123 N. Beacon St.
Boston, MA 02135
Parts, accessories, anti-theft

H&H Specialties, Inc.
20 Reid Road
Chelmsford, MA 01824
Wheels, chassis parts

Maryland
Artomate
Box 172
Cockeysville, MD 21030
Softite lug nut sockets

Minnesota
Karrousel Racing, Inc.
5213 W. Broadway
Minneapolis, MN 55429
Accessories, suspension kits

Missouri
In Gear
8328 Olive Blvd.
Olivette, MO 63132
Porsche T-shirts

Imparts
2535 S. Brentwood Blvd.
St. Louis, MO 63144
Parts, accessories, tools

Mathis Marketing
517 Paul Ave.
Florissant, MO 63031
Wheels

New Jersey
Kleban Suspension Systems
40 Railroad Ave.
Hackensack, NJ 07601
Bilstein shock absorbers

Stable Energies
2207 Rt. 4 East
Fort Lee, NJ 07024
911 & 924 camber truss

JCM
198 Route 206 South
Somerville, NJ 08876
Tire chains

New York
Porsche Perfect
554 W. 38th St.
New York, NY 10018
Custom modifications, accessories

The Great Sheep Company
93 N. Park Avenue
Rockville Centre, NY 11570
Sheepskin seat covers

Zelenda Machine and Tools Corp.
66-02 Austin St.
Forest Hills, NY 11374
Service tools for Porsches

Formula Garage
1868 Utica Ave.
Brooklyn, NY 11234
Competition preparation

Barnes Publishing
Box 323
Scarsdale, NY 10583
Brian Redman Porsche 917 posters

Porsche Auto Recyclers
58 Townsend St.
Port Chester, NY 10573
Purchase & sale of Porsche parts

Kolin Industries, Inc.
59P-4 West Pondfield Rd.
Bronxville, NY 10708
Car theft alarms

Dorf-Weber
Blydenburgh Road
Hauppauge, NY 11787
Restoration

North Carolina
Coachcraft
P.O. Box 728
Moorseville, NC 28115
Used Porsche parts

Gene Garner Automotive, Inc.
1324 Roanoke Ave.
Roanoke Rapids, NC 27870
Repairs, restoration

Ohio
MAH
6660 Busch Blvd.
Columbus, OH 43229
Parts, accessories

Stoddard Imported Cars, Inc.
38845 Mentor Ave.
Willoughby, OH 44094-0908
Parts, accessories, restoration

Vic & Walts
2510 Triplett Blvd.
Akron, OH 44312
Exhaust systems

Wheels of Art
Box 289
Worthington, OH 43085
356, 911, 928 art lithographs

Sachs
909 Crocker Road
Westlake, OH 44145
Shock absorbers

J.J.R. Products Co.
P.O. Box 532
Hartville, OH 44632
914 stainless rocker panels

Racequip
809 Phillipi Rd.
Columbus, OH 43228
Parts & accessories

Classic Cravats
4154 Skyview Dr. Suite 127
Brownswick, OH 44212
Porsche ties

Oregon
Inlines Sportswear
2311 E. Burnside
Portland, OR 97214
Clothing

Quickor Engineering
6710 S.W. 111 Ave.
Beaverton, OR 97005
Chassis performance parts

Monte's Motors
1638 W. Burnside St.
Portland, OR 97207
U-joint replacements

Pennsylvania
Subtle Dynamics
215 Plank Ave.
Paoli, PA 19301
Accessories, engine parts, books

Sewickley Porsche Audi Alfa
Ohio River Blvd. & Chestnut St.
Sewickley, PA 15143
Porsche gifts

Seat Skins, Inc.
P.O. Box 273
Newtown, PA 18940
Sheepskin seat covers

Holbert Racing
1425 Easton Rd.
Warrington, PA 18976
Porsche 924 specialists

Texas
Jones Autowerkes
1134 97th St.
San Antonio, TX 78214
Complete Porsche restoration

McDougall's Carrera Automotive
86 Haby Dr.
San Antonio, TX 78212
Restoration, service, parts

Zim & Mayo
1804 Reliance Parkway
Bedford, TX 76021
Porsche specialists

Tom Knoblauch
12140 Potranco Rd.
San Antonio, TX 78253
Solid gold Porsche emblem

Nine-Eleven Enterprises, Inc.
2750 Northaven, Suite 207
Dallas, TX 75229
Parts & accessories

Utah
Alta Classics
220 W. Central Ave., Suite 15
Salt Lake City, UT 84107
Porsche 356 reconditioned parts

Classic Specialties
8137 Mountain Oaks Dr.
Salt Lake City, UT 84121
Alloy wheels

Virginia
Electrodyne
2316 Jefferson Davis Hwy.
Alexandria, VA 22313
Parts, accessories

Koni America
P.O. Box 40
Culpepper, VA 22701
Shock absorbers

Randy Owens
385 Courthouse Road
Vienna, VA 22180
Porsche artwork, serigraphs

Wisconsin
Classic Motorbooks, Inc.
P.O. Box 1
Osceola, WI 54020
Porsche books

Porsche clubs

Australia
Porsche Club Canberra
c/o Terry Lovett
57 Kinkead St.
Evatt 2617 A.C.T., Australia

Porsche Club of New South Wales
19 Owen St.
Lindfield 2070
Sydney, N.S.W., Australia

Porsche Club of Queensland
14 Fairley St. Indooroopilly
Brisbane 4068
Queensland, Australia

Porsche Owners Club of South
Australia
88, Valley View Drive
Highbury, South Australia 5089

Porsche Club of Victoria
P.O. Box 222
Kew, Victoria, Australia 3101

Austria
Porsche Club Osterreich
Stelzhamerstrasse 19a
4600 Weis, Austria

Belgium
Porsche Club Belgique
50, rue du Mail
1050 Bruxelles, Belgium

Porsche 356 Club de Belgique
110 rue Essegem
1090 Bruxelles, Belgium

Denmark
Porsche Club Danmark
6 Yvelvej 4
29425 Icodsborg, Denmark

Federal Republic of Germany
Porsche Club of America
c/o Ron Randolph
Hainer Weg 12
6072 Gotxenhain, West Germany

Porsche Carrera RS IG
c/o Wilfried Holzenthal
Haupstrasse 36
5419 Weidenhahn, West Germany

Porsche Club Deutschland
Podbielskiallee 25–27
1000 Berlin 33, West Germany

Porsche 356 Euroclub e.V.
Markgrafenstrasse 2
4300 Essen 1, West Germany

Porsche 356
Interessengemeinschaft
Bergeracker 30
5210 Troisdorf, West Germany

Porsche 914–6 Club
c/o Joseph Reip
Durerstrasse 38
5020 Frechen-Konigsdorf,
West Germany

Finland
Porsche Club Suomi-Finnland
Sipilan Kartano
12380 Leppakoski, Finland

France
Porsche Club de France
c/o Sonauto SA
1, Ave du Fief BP 479
95005 Cergy Pontoise Cedex,
France

356 Porsche Club de France
21 bis Rue Volta
FR–31000 Toulouse, France

Great Britain
356 Register
Rookery Lodge
181 Stanmore Hill
Stanmore, Middlesex, England

Porsche Club Great Britain
64 Raisins Hill
Pinner, Middlesex, England

Hong Kong
Porsche Club Hong Kong
924–926, Cheung Sha Wan Road
Kowlon, Hong Kong

Italy
Porsche Club Italia
Via Carlo Osma, 2
20151 Milano, Italy

Porsche Carrera Italia Sud
Corso Trieste, 83
81100 Caserta, Italy

Japan
Porsche Club of Japan
c/o Mitsuwa Motors Co. Ltd.
No. 18–6 Roppongi 3–Chome
Minato-ku
Tokyo 106, Japan

Luxembourg
Porsche Club Luxembourg
c/o Novotel
Route d'Echternach
Luxembourg/Dommeldange
Luxembourg

Netherlands
Porsche 356 Club Nederland
Postfach 356
NL-Someren 5710, Holland

Porsche Club Holland
Wim Sonneveldlaan 227
3584 ZS Utrecht, Holland

Nederlandse Porsche Club
Dorpsstaat 171
6871 AJ Renkum, Holland

Norway
Porsche Klubb Norge
Postboks 32
Lysejordet
Oslo 7, Norway

New Zealand
Porsche Club of New Zealand
204 Beach Road
Campbells Bay
Auckland 10, New Zealand

South Africa
Porsche Club of South Africa
P.O. Box 9834
Johannesburg 2000, South Africa

Sweden
Porsche Club Sverige
Box 34025
10026 Stockholm, Sweden

Porsche 356 Klubb Sverige
Sparogatan 5
SE-25372 Helsingborg, Sweden

Switzerland
Ostschweizerischer Porsche Club
Rorschacherstrasse 139
9000 St. Gallen, Switzerland

Porsche 356 Club Schweiz
Zweierestrasse 13
5443 Niederrohrdorf, Switzerland

Porsche 914 Club Schweiz
Wilerstrasse 30
9542 Munchwilen TG, Switzerland

United States
Porsche Owners Club
P.O. Box 54910 Terminal Annex
Los Angeles, CA 90054

356 Registry
P.O. Box 07845
Columbus, Ohio 43207

Black Porsche, Inc.
P.O. Box 951
Oakland, CA 94604

Porsche 914–6 Club USA
c/o Larry A. Morris
Alan Johnson Racing, Inc.
5220 Gaines St.
San Diego, CA 92110

Ruth Harte
Porsche Club of America*
PO Box 10402
Alexandria, VA 22310

* The Porsche Club of America has
127 regions in the U.S. and Canada.
The address listed is for the club's
current president, Hank Malter. A
letter to Hank can get you the
address and phone number of the
region closest to you.